OUR GHOSTS

Our Ghosts

Sally Stubbs

SCIROCCO DRAMA

Our Ghosts
first published 2021 by Scirocco Drama
An imprint of J. Gordon Shillingford Publishing Inc.

Scirocco Drama Editor: Glenda MacFarlane
Cover design by Doowah Design
Author photo by Matt Reznek
Production photos Zachary Tanner

Search and rescue photos by WSAR volunteers;
logbook photo by Jay Gooch;
Stubbs family photos enhanced by Mitsuru Naga.

Printed and bound in Canada on 100% post-consumer recycled paper.
We acknowledge the financial support of the Manitoba Arts Council and
The Canada Council for the Arts for our publishing program.

Production inquiries to:
Catherine Knights
catherine@catalysttcm.com

Library and Archives Canada Cataloguing in Publication

Title: Our ghosts / Sally Stubbs.
Names: Stubbs, Sally, author.
Description: A play.
Identifiers: Canadiana 20210136774 | ISBN 9781927922750 (softcover)
Classification: LCC PS8637.T86 O97 2021 | DDC C812/.6—dc23

J. Gordon Shillingford Publishing
P.O. Box 86, RPO Corydon Avenue, Winnipeg, MB Canada R3M 3S3

In loving memory of my mom,

Claire Stubbs,

Gerald Stubbs,

the father I never knew,

and Jerry Stubbs,

the brother I lost.

Sally Stubbs

A multi-award-winning playwright and educator, Sally also directs, performs and produces. Most recently,Underbelly, her first TV pilot, was a semi-finalist in Table Read My Screenplay Genre Competition and her first screenplay, *Doors & Windows,* was honoured as Best Short Screenplay, World Webfest Mania, Fall 2020. Her plays, published by Scirocco Drama, have been presented in Canada, Sweden, India, South Africa and the USA. Sally's new script, *Our Ghosts,* was livestreamed as part of #CanadaPerforms / National Arts Centre on May 2, 2020; received its initial production at Western Edge Theatre, Nanaimo, BC in October / November 2019; and was an official selection of the 2018 Women Playwrights International Conference in Santiago, Chile. Work in process: a collaboration on *Polly & the Penthouse: A Spirited Musical; Underbelly,* a TV pilot inspired by Canada's first women police officers and her script *And Bella Sang with Us*; and webisodes adapted from her play, *Centurions*. As part of The Centurions Project team, Sally is currently working on *Speak Up, Centurions!* (working title), a documentary made possible thanks to COVID-19 Emergency funding awarded by Canada Council for the Arts. Sally is particularly proud to have received a Prime Minister's Award for her work with theatre and youth.

Sally received her B.A., B.Ed., M.A. (Art History) and M.F.A. (Creative Writing) from the University of Victoria, and trained and performed in theatre in Canada, the USA and the UK. She is a co-founder and senior advisor of The CASA Award, a Canadian and South African partnership between The Playwrights Guild of Canada's Women's Caucus and The African Women Playwrights Network, which creates funding opportunities for women-identified playwrights living in South Africa. She served for three years as Women's Caucus Chair and Editor for the Playwrights Guild of Canada. Sally has twice acted as a Jessie Theatre Awards juror. She has served on the boards of both Touchstone Theatre and Playwrights' Theatre Centre.

www.sallystubbswriter.com www.thecenturionsproject.ca

Acknowledgements

Thanks to the many dedicated people and organizations that have over many years been working to solve the mystery of the disappearance of Flying Officers Gerald Stephen Stubbs (my father) and his co-pilot, James E. Miller. They include: Brad Sills, President of Whistler Search and Rescue Society, and the volunteer members; Steve LeClair, recently retired from Whistler RCMP; the Resort Municipality of Whistler; *Pique Newsmagazine* (for edition 22.45 November 12, 2015, Still Searching); *Call Out* Search and Rescue Season III, Episode 1, CALLOUTSAR.TV.

Thanks to: Sherry Walker who, as a child, sighted and reported the T-33 on March 22, 1956; and new friends, Michele Miller, Flying Officer Miller's daughter, and her husband, Ian.

My heartfelt thanks to dear friends, relations, and colleagues who, for years or decades, have witnessed the impact of the mystery of my father's disappearance on my family — especially Mom — and been there for us. Finally, love and thanks to my partner, Rod, for his enduring love and support and his determination to help me put this mystery to bed.

Foreword

The Space of Absence

Sally Stubbs and I first met up in a coffee shop not far from Kitsilano Beach and she unveiled to me an early draft of the mystery of her missing father. This absence has formed and tracked like a ghost through her life. I was in awe of this incredible tale, in awe of Sally's bravery in telling it, and I was hooked. When I think back to that first meeting, I am struck by what a journey it has been, involving the input of so many artists. From my first read I understood how profound this play is for Sally, and as a director and dramaturge I saw the opportunity it contains for a profound response from an audience. Every play a writer pens is like a child: something they labour over, care for, bring into the world to face love and criticism. When the story is so personal, and not only personal but spanning a writer's entire life, it is difficult to encapsulate that level of importance. What I am most struck by in looking at the intervening years is the level of detailed work Sally has put into *Our Ghosts*. The true work of a playwright is not in dashing the idea down on paper, but in reworking, rewriting, carving, crafting, honing. Eliminating things when they don't work, yes, absolutely. But really working an idea to the fullest expression of its possibility before doing so. Trying to untie the knot rather than cutting the string. What I have been fortunate enough to bear witness to in Sally Stubbs' work on *Our Ghosts* is her willingness to dig in and do that work. To take the truth and apply it to the dramatic form: to utilize metaphor and a craftsperson's lens to bring key elements forward. To imagine people who are the closest to her on earth — including herself as character — and to work them to their fullest dramatic potential while still being true to their real identity. That is the "wright" of playwright: not just the creation, but the construction, the repair. Sally had a beautiful play those years ago, but her dedication, determination, and hard work have taken it even further than I imagined.

I also had the good fortune to work with Sally on this piece during the darkest initial days of the COVID-19 pandemic. I say fortune because the opportunity to continue making theatre, making excellent, text-based theatre, helped all of us involved to believe that there would be an end to the restrictions and that important work like this would find its way into theatres again. We produced a reading as part of #CanadaPerforms at the National Arts Centre in which all the performers acted from the safety of their own homes and came together for a livestream via Zoom and YouTube. The response to the piece was incredible. People loved it. They loved the nature of a true unsolved mystery woven into a complex and challenging family drama. There is an understanding in the concept of ghosts that we all share, regardless of whether that identification is literal or figurative. The idea that people from our past stay with us in some form, that their story never stops weaving into our own, and that their memory can be both a burden and a gift is universal, even as the details of this story are unusual and surprising. This piece reached people, people burdened by the pandemic, and reillumined their imaginations.

My imagination is set alight most profoundly in this piece during a late scene between Stevie and Kate. The two are debating what their life would have been if their father had lived. The gap between the life they want and the mom they want is the space in which all their dreams lie. It is so easy and heartbreaking to understand: you simply can't have it both ways.

I feel infinitely grateful that Sally shared her story and her heart with me in inviting me to be part of the process of *Our Ghosts*. I think that is one of the major reasons that audiences respond to this play the way that they do. They understand that she is sharing her heart with them, too. And it is a beautiful gift.

Rachel Peake, director, dramaturge, and creator
January 2021

Production History

Our Ghosts received its first production by Western Edge Theatre at Harbour City Theatre in Nanaimo, BC on October 25, 2019 with the following cast:

KATE SWANSON .... Terry Lynn Boyle

MOIRA SWANSON .... Clarice McCord

STEVIE, VIC, SCOTTY,
FELIX, CHRIS SEERS .... Darrian Gaetz

LIEUTENANT LORRAINE,
COMMANDER BUCKLES,
TONY LEON, BEAR .... Brian March

ARCHIE RAINS .... Ted Girard

WIND .... Melissa Kahan

Directed by .... Wendy Wearne
Lighting Design & Operator........................ Erik Tully
Sound Design .... David Bourne
Set Design...................................... Michael Armstrong
Costume Design.................................. Lorna McLellan
Videographer... Jeff Monson
Stage Manager, Sound
Operator, Video Design .... Amy MacFarlane
Assistant Stage Manager .... Melissa Kahan
Artistic Director... Brian March
Executive Director .... Frank Moher

Development History

I gratefully acknowledge the support of: BC Arts Council; City of Richmond Artist in Residence Program 2015; TheatreOne; Western Edge Theatre; The Canadian Play Thing; #CanadaPerforms, National Arts Centre / Centre national des Arts; Firehall Arts Centre; Arts Club Theatre; Belfry Theatre; Western Gold Theatre.

For their insights and enthusiastic support during this epic writing process, my thanks to: Sherry MacDonald, Rachel Peake, Barbara Pollard, Wet Ink Collective, Leslie Stark, The Tarts, Colleen Murphy, Rachel Ditor, Veronique West, Michael Shamata, Nicolle Nattrass, Tanja Dixon-Warren and Seamus Fera.

Our Ghosts received dramaturgical support, workshops and / or public readings in Vancouver, Victoria and Nanaimo, BC. Following the show's premiere and rewrites in 2020, two exciting, livestreamed presentations were directed by Rachel Peake for The Canadian Play Thing and as part of #CanadaPerforms, National Arts Centre / Centre national des Arts. It was named an official selection of the 2018 Women Playwrights International Conference (Santiago, Chile) and was a semi-finalist for the Ashland New Play Festival.

Thanks to the many artists who contributed to the script's development: director / dramaturgs Chelsea Haberlin, Nicolle Nattrass and Rachel Peake; actors Corina Akeson, Sebastien Archibald, Michael Armstrong, Jennifer Clements, Craig Erickson, Genevieve Fleming, Adrian Hough, Megan Leitch, Nicola Lipman, Tamara McCarthy, Susinn Macfarlane, David Mann, France Perras, Tom Pickett, Barbara Pollard, Robert Salvadore, and Raugi Yu; designers Joelysa Panakaea, John Webber and Stephanie Wong; poster designers David Botton and John Endo Greenaway.

And to the team at Western Edge Theatre for bringing such generosity and heart to the first production of *Our Ghosts.*

As always, my thanks to my agent, Catherine Knights. And my ongoing admiration and gratitude to the fine folks at Scirocco Drama, particularly publisher Karen Haughian and editor Glenda MacFarlane.

Characters

KATE SWANSON

62, only surviving family member in the present. It becomes clear as the play progresses that she is talking to her mum.

MOIRA SWANSON

Kate's mother. Played by two actors:

MOIRA (in her 60s to 90)

Moira is 90 in 2016.

YOUNG MOIRA (from 29 to mid-40s), i.e., scenes 4, 5, 6, 7, 13 (for Stevie's 16th birthday) and 14. These scenes take place on the Comox Base, in Winnipeg and in Victoria with teenage Kate and Stevie.

In the present — October 23, 2017 — MOIRA has been dead for a year. In her later years, there are some indications of early dementia, but she never forgets Vic or the details and fallout relating to his disappearance.

STEVIE

Kate's brother, Moira's son, early 30s when he dies. A ghost. He appears at different ages during the play. Is seen only by Kate.

VIC

Kate's father, Moira's husband. Disappeared in his early 30s. A ghost seen only by Moira.

LIEUTENANT LORRAINE, SCOTTY, COMMANDER BUCKLES, FELIX (RCAF 2016 & 1956)

CHRIS SEERS

Head of Whistler Search and Rescue, appears
Oct 2016 & 2017

MARY, MR. WELLS & MR. THORNE

Voices heard by Kate.
Mary is 8 in 1956 and 71 in 2017.

WIND

A force of nature — and a supernatural force — Wind is often present and active in the storytelling. It drives most transitions and has lines in the scene on the mountain. I suggest the actor playing Stevie and Vic appears to give voice to Wind in the mountain scene.

GRIZZLY BEAR

A messenger. Suggest light, shadow and sound to bring to life.

Casting: 3 women, 2 men:

KATE

MOIRA, MARY (voice only)

YOUNG MOIRA, MRS. WELLS (voice only), SEARCHER (voice only)

STEVIE, VIC, *FELIX (see second suggestion below), MR. THORNE (voice only), WIND (on the mountain), GRIZZLY BEAR (sound only)

LIEUTENANT LORRAINE (Québécois), SCOTTY, COMMANDER BUCKLES, CHRIS SEERS, *FELIX (possible with an obvious, lightning-quick transformation)

Production Notes

Inspired by the mysterious disappearance of the playwright's pilot-father in a routine flight, and its impact on those left behind, *Our Ghosts* is at once a taut investigative tale, a moving testament to the love and tenacity of a woman determined to uncover the truth, and a journey toward learning to live with our ghosts.

Setting & Set

Kate conjures the world of the play from her mother's stories and memories, letters, photographs, and documents; her own memories, imaginings, and writing; and their ghosts. As is the case with deep memories, imagination and "haunting," there is some jumping about as one thought or emotion inspires or intrudes upon another.

When Kate is alone and talking in the present, she is addressing her mother. It may not be immediately obvious to the audience, and that is fine.

The "now" of the play is October 23, 2017, when Kate is in Moira's empty home: the first anniversary of Moira's death. The story travels to: Moira and Vic's home in Married Quarters on the Comox Air Base, BC and then to Winnipeg in 1956; Moira's modest home in Victoria, late 1960s, early 1970s and primarily in October 2016 and 2017; the wild Callaghan Lake country in BC's Whistler Mountain area in October 2016 and October 2017.

This is not a naturalistic play. Set must be minimalist and flexible to incorporate fluid movement between space, time, and realities. Light, shadow, and sound will play primary roles in bringing the world of the play to life. Transitions must be clean and fluid. WIND is often driving those transitions. There must be no blackouts between scenes.

Character Notes

Our Ghosts has been written for five actors: three women and two men. It is possible to stage the play with four actors: two women, two men. In each case, all actors playing more than one character must be able to transform believably and quickly, yet subtly. If only one actor plays Moira from 28 to 90 years of age, the ability to transform subtly is especially important to ensure believability and clarity of story. Casting for five outlined below.

Kate appears in her memories and stories, but always as she is in the present. For example, in the most extreme case: when she spends time with her young mother on the Comox Base, Kate is participating in events told to her by Moira. Kate DOES NOT become a toddler when she steps into those scenes. The playwright suggests that Moira interacts with a "mimed" toddler-Kate. This was effective in the Western Edge Theatre production. Kate, meanwhile, responds verbally to her mum as the woman she is, not the child she was.

In the present, Kate is the only member of her family still alive. Thus, actions of her family members, as she recollects and conjures, may transcend the realities and limitations of living beings.

Production Notes

When indicated in dialogue, "/" means speakers overlap; "—" means the next speaker picks up right away; "..." means that actors are reacting without dialogue.

Lieutenant should be pronounced "Leftenant" (traditional Canadian pronunciation) rather than the American "Lootenant."

Our Ghosts runs 95 - 100 minutes.

Prologue

In shadow, a couple — YOUNG MOIRA and VIC in their earliest days together — dance a wild, uninhibited jitterbug. Music shifts. They slow-dance and appear to become one as YOUNG MOIRA says the following to VIC.

YOUNG MOIRA: Lock step. Lock hips. Lock lips.

Scene One

It's October 23, 2017, mid-afternoon. KATE is alone in MOIRA's home, recently sold and just about empty. Spread around her: files, letters, documents, a journal, boxes of photographs. She picks up an old black and white photograph.

KATE: The Pink House. That's what we called it. *(Remembering.)* The sky is cloudless, blazing. I must be three. I can't be four. We're still in Winnipeg. I'm sitting on the front steps of The Pink House, alone, waiting. I'm wearing a little blue dress with smocking across the chest and short puffy sleeves. I love this dress. I'm shifting my bare feet back and forth and curling up my toes because they're burning on the concrete steps. There's the roar of the bus. The brakes squeal and it stops across the street. When it pulls away, there you are. I wave and shout and hop-run across the burning road, grab your hand and, that's it. My first memory.

Beat.

KATE: It's 3:00 a.m., a little over a year ago. October 2nd, 2016. I'm right here, standing at this window, waiting. Where the hell are you?

Immediately: the sound of shrieking WIND and branches scraping against the house. 90-year-old MOIRA appears leaning into the WIND. She's barelegged, barefoot, wearing only a knee-length flannelette nightgown speckled with holes and streaks of dried blood. A leather parachute harness bearing the weight of a man swings from a tree and groans in the WIND. Text below overlaps.

MOIRA: I'm coming, sweetheart!

KATE: Oh no.

MOIRA: *(Calling to "others.")* Over here! / You're never going to find him on the ground. Look up. Look up. Look up!

KATE: No. No. No. No. No. No. No.

MOIRA: *(Calling.)* Hurry! We've got to get him down!

A flashlight beam illuminates MOIRA, then KATE is with her.

MOIRA: Get that light out of my eyes.

KATE: / Mum, please.

MOIRA: Where are the rest of your searchers? He's up there.

KATE: It'll be the wind or a raccoon. Those buggers are everywhere. Let's get you inside before you freeze to death.

And they're in MOIRA's house.

KATE: Home. See? In your living room. Grampa's old armchair, your TV, boxes and boxes and more boxes, me.

MOIRA: Vic was here, Kate.

KATE: No.

MOIRA: He's here now.

KATE: You were sleepwalking.

MOIRA: I was awake. I heard the wind in the trees. I was young and not young.

KATE: Time for bed. Big day tomorrow.

MOIRA: *(Remembering.)* Yes. That Lieutenant fella…

KATE: Lieutenant Lorraine.

MOIRA: Lorraine. Yes, that's it. He's bringing news.

KATE: And so you've wound yourself up like the Tasmanian Devil.

MOIRA: I don't know any Tasmanian Devil.

KATE: *The Bugs Bunny Show*. You used to say the Tasmanian Devil was Stevie's mentor.

MOIRA: Stevie?

KATE: My brother. Your son.

MOIRA: I know who Stevie is.

KATE: Yeah, well, sometimes you forget things.

MOIRA: Not my son.

KATE: Fine, good, I'm sorry. All I was trying to say is, you wind yourself up too tight, you break.

MOIRA: I know what I know.

KATE: Let's get you back to your bed.

MOIRA: I can't sleep up there.

KATE: You can try.

MOIRA: I can't breathe up there. Let go of me.

KATE: Done.

MOIRA: *(On a mission.)* Papers.

KATE: Not now.

MOIRA: The Lieutenant fella will want to see these.

KATE: I don't think so.

MOIRA: Have they found Vic?

KATE: How the hell would I know?

MOIRA: Oh god, what if…? Deal with that when it comes, /Moira.

KATE: Slow down. You're going to fall.

MOIRA: Might put me out of my misery. Give you a little peace.

KATE: Tempting.

MOIRA: I beg your pardon?

KATE: Just kidding. /I think.

MOIRA: You can be some bitch when you set your mind to it, Katie Swanson.

KATE: It's in my genes, Ma. *(Exiting.)* I'll get your robe and slippers. Then we'll sort out a bed for you down here. God, the blood on your nightgown.

MOIRA: *(Calling after KATE.)* All night, scratch, scratch, scratch.

KATE: *(Returning with MOIRA's robe, slippers, bedding.)* Blood on your robe, too.

MOIRA: Feel this. Feel.

KATE: Stop scratching.

MOIRA: Skin like paper. Tears at the slightest touch. Soon I'll slide out of it. Like an old snake.

KATE: You're making it worse. *(Exiting.)* Where are the bandages?

MOIRA: Kitchen. Or bathroom.

KATE: *(Entering.)* There must be thirty empty pill bottles on that counter. Arm, please. Holy crap. You got a licence for these fingernails? You could decapitate somebody.

MOIRA: Better mind your manners then, kid. *(Searching.)* Cigarette. *(Finds, lights up.)* My closest and most constant life companions.

KATE: Thanks a heap. Put this stuff on.

MOIRA: Take these papers, keep them safe.

KATE: *(Helping MOIRA into robe and slippers.)* Put this on. You're trembling.

MOIRA: *(About papers.)* This is our evidence, ammunition. You're going to need this when I'm gone. It'll be up to you then.

KATE: Not now. I'm so tired I'm dizzy.

MOIRA: They may have found your father. Does that mean anything to you?

KATE: Of course it does, but Mum, please, it's after three o'clock in the fucking morning.

MOIRA: Language.

KATE: You remember I was in Vancouver when you called, right? That Alec and I actually live there.

MOIRA: Is Alec home?

KATE: Until next week. Then he's working in Toronto for a couple of weeks.

MOIRA: Your lovely man never stays still. But you, you're on holiday.

KATE: Leave of absence. And just because I'm not teaching right now doesn't mean I'm not working.

MOIRA: You can write your little stories anywhere.

KATE: Good to know.

MOIRA: *(About a photo.)* Your dad and me in Gimli.

KATE: I'm going to make up a bed for you right here on the couch.

MOIRA: Vic's starting to get plump around the edges here. My biscuits and gravy man. We met in Winnipeg after the war. At the train station. I'd been home on leave from Camp Shilo, that's east of Brandon, Manitoba. When you work in payroll during a war you're the last to get discharged. Your Uncle Gerry came to see me off and brought Vic along.

Sound of trains shunting in a station. VIC appears.

MOIRA: *(To VIC.)* There you are. *(To KATE.)* They met overseas. Gerry was a gunner.

KATE: Uh huh.

MOIRA: They lost touch when the war ended, then ran into each other in a beer parlour in the Winnipeg Exchange District. Glorious coincidence. Your uncle made an ass of himself on booze in those days. Most of them did. Vic not so much. Your father was a pilot.

KATE: Bed's made up.

MOIRA: He stayed on with the Air Force. Took it seriously. All of it. One of the best. They all said so.

Vic sits down beside me on a bench in the station and the three of us share the chicken salad sandwiches Mum packed for my journey. He seems nice enough, but I guess you could say his effect on me is a slow, steady burn, not a sudden jolt to the heart. I notice things, though. He listens, not everyone does that. He's really hearing me, seeing me, not just Gerry's little sister. And his lips. Dear lord, Vic has the most beautiful, full lips I have ever seen on a man, on anyone.

KATE: Why don't you get under these covers?

MOIRA: There's a tiny crumb of bread on his bottom lip. I can't stop myself. I've never done anything like this before, I mean I've just met the man, but I reach out with one finger and—

MOIRA extends her arm as if to brush that crumb off VIC's lip.

MOIRA: Gerry makes some asinine comment, the train arrives and soon I'm waving to them from the window. Vic writes me, just friendly "How are you? This is what I did today" letters. / And when I finally finish up at Camp Shilo and head home, there he is. Waiting for me at the station. He takes my bag and my hand.

KATE: And when I finally finish up at Camp Shilo and head home, there he is. Waiting for me at the station. He takes my bag and my hand. And the rest is history. Let me tuck you in.

VIC disappears. MOIRA lights another cigarette.

KATE: Give me that smoke and get into bed.

MOIRA: I will not.

KATE: Fine. I'm going up to bed before I expire. But if you're planning to be awake for your meeting tomorrow, you'll put that damn cigarette out right now and get to sleep. Good night.

MOIRA: Take that mountain of files.

KATE: I thought Lieutenant Lorraine needed to see this stuff.

MOIRA: I have copies.

KATE: Of course you do, and I don't want them, thank you / very much.

MOIRA: Tough. Keep them safe. And read them.

KATE: I've read—

MOIRA: Every, single page.

KATE: I'm not talking about this now.

MOIRA: You're welcome to that box of photos, too.

KATE: Good night.

MOIRA: There are some nice ones of Stevie in there.

This stops KATE. She pulls a photo out of the box.

KATE: Oh god. Who knew he ever looked like this?

KATE hears STEVIE's mischievous little chant. It's haunting, as if coming from far away.

STEVIE'S VOICE: Uh eee uh uh eee uh eee
Musical notes: C G Eflat D Eflat C G (Octave below first G.)

Uh eee uh uh eee uh.
C G Eflat D Eflat C

KATE: *(To MOIRA.)* You must want to keep these.

MOIRA: Look around you. And a lifetime of boxes upstairs.

KATE: But Stevie—

MOIRA: I prefer the images playing in my head. They keep me marching.

KATE: Is Stevie playing in your head now?

MOIRA looks at another photograph of her life with VIC.

MOIRA: Look at the bottles on this table. Like a distillery. Rye, rum, Scotch, /beer, mixer.

KATE: Do I ever play in there?

MOIRA: Vic was the only sober man at that table. Where the hell do you think you're going?

KATE snaps the light off and exits with the box of photographs.

MOIRA: Turn that light on!

Scene Two

And it's the next morning. KATE is looking through the box of photos of STEVIE. She hears his voice again.

STEVIE'S VOICE: Uh eee uh uh eee uh eee
Uh eee uh uh eee uh.

KATE: Little bugger.

And there's a knocking and MOIRA, still in her dressing gown, is opening the front door.

MOIRA: Oh lord, I, I… Is it that time already?

LORRAINE: Mrs. /Swanson?

MOIRA: Kate?

LORRAINE: I'm Lieutenant Xavier—

MOIRA shuts the door. Knocking begins again. MOIRA comes to find KATE.

MOIRA: *(Gasping for breath.)* Kate?

KATE: Have you been up all night?

MOIRA: Yes!

KATE: Are you trying to kill yourself?

MOIRA: Get the door.

KATE: I thought you were doing that.

MOIRA: I need to put on my face.

KATE: I'd start with clothes if I /were you.

MOIRA: The door, smartass.

KATE: Calm down.

MOIRA: Calm down? This is no day / for calm.

KATE: I'm gonna get you a pill.

MOIRA: Stuff the pill. The Air Force is here!

MOIRA exits, and KATE is at the door with LIEUTENANT LORRAINE of the RCAF.

LORRAINE: The lady I just met, saw, she is Mrs. Moira Swanson?

KATE: Yes.

LORRAINE: May I speak with her?

KATE: She's dying to speak to you, but, well, she's just—

MOIRA: *(Calling.)* Kate!

KATE: On second thought, I think she's ready for us. I should warn you though. She's wound up right to the ceiling.

LORRAINE: You are worried.

KATE: Yes.

LORRAINE: It is better I come back another time?

MOIRA: Kate!

KATE: *(To MOIRA.)* In a minute. *(To LORRAINE.)* No. It's got to be today. We are not going through this again.

And KATE and LORRAINE are with MOIRA. VIC hovers nearby.

KATE: Mum, Lieutenant Xavier Lorraine.

MOIRA: Come in, come in.

LORRAINE: Thank you for seeing me, Mrs. Swanson.

MOIRA: Would you like some coffee or tea?

LORRAINE: No, thank you.

MOIRA: It's no trouble. Kate, make us some coffee.

LORRAINE: I think it is better we should—

MOIRA: I bet you want to know all about my Vic.

LORRAINE: I do know a little about Flying Officers Swanson and James, too, / from the file.

MOIRA: *(Showing photo.)* We're in Gimli, Manitoba here.

LORRAINE: A fine-looking couple.

MOIRA: We met in Winnipeg after the war. At the train / station.

KATE: Mum, I'm sure Lieutenant Lorraine has a very busy schedule. Maybe we should listen to what he has to say.

MOIRA: Yes, yes. Of course.

LORRAINE: Very good. I will get right to it then.

MOIRA: Straight to the point.

LORRAINE: I am here because the fuselage — that's the body of fighter jet T-33 454 — has been located.

MOIRA: Oh lord oh lord / oh lord, I knew it!

KATE: Slow down and hang onto me. How? Where?

LORRAINE: Mrs. Swanson, you would like to sit?

MOIRA: No. No. I couldn't.

LORRAINE: The site was discovered by a civilian helicopter pilot flying over rugged terrain in the Lake Callaghan area.

KATE: So it's not too far from where that hiker found the canopy way back in, uh—

MOIRA: 1974.

LORRAINE: Yes. Not too far, you are right.

KATE: When?

LORRAINE: August 7.

KATE: But that's weeks ago. Why are we just hearing this now?

LORRAINE: It's a complicated and lengthy process.

KATE: Believe me, we know.

LORRAINE: An official team, convened by the Directorate of Flight Safety, began a formal accident investigation on August the 9th. Specific components from the site were removed.

KATE: What kinds of components?

MOIRA: Let the Lieutenant finish.

LORRAINE: We're not at liberty to comment on specifics of an ongoing investigation. But I can say these components were taken for analysis in our facility in Ottawa.

MOIRA: My husband.

LORRAINE: Yes. Mrs. Swanson, uh, I regret that, uh, that we have been unable to find any trace of the ejection seats. Or of either pilot.

MOIRA: No. No. That can't be. No no/no no no...

VIC disappears.

MOIRA: *(To VIC.)* Don't leave me!

KATE: Mum, I've got you.

LORRAINE: Mrs. Swanson, Kate, on behalf of the Canadian Armed Forces and the Department of National Defence, please accept—

MOIRA: Is this never going to end?

KATE: Oh, it's going to end. You have my word on it. Why did the plane crash?

LORRAINE: I'm unable to say at this time.

KATE: Who makes these decisions?

LORRAINE: This is Department of National Defence procedure.

MOIRA: Let me tell you how your procedure has served my family, Lieutenant Lor... Lor... Lorry. Fifty-nine years ago, fifty-nine /years

KATE: Mum, please—

MOIRA: When my Katie here and her newborn brother, Stephen, and I were forced from our home on the Comox Base I, I, I—

KATE: Sit down. /Try to calm down.

MOIRA: I received a solemn promise that I would be the first to know if any trace of that plane was found.

LORRAINE: Your daughter is right, Mrs. Swanson. Let me help you—

MOIRA: I will not sit down, calm down, lie down! Not until I know everything. What? Why? How? Where? Eighteen years later that hiker discovered the jet's canopy. And nobody, nobody, not one goddamn soul in your Ministry thought to tell me that my husband's plane came down over land. That he hadn't become fish food.

LORRAINE: I'm sure they told you what they were at liberty to—

MOIRA: Not a bit of it! I didn't learn until 1991. Seventeen years after the canopy was found. And then only because I finally got my hands on the incident file. After thirty-five years of nagging and scrapping and pleading with bureaucrats I read about that canopy in a goddamn file.

KATE: Let your breath out. Out.

LORRAINE: I'm sorry.

MOIRA: No, not good enough, young man. I've been hearing those two words since I lost my love… and… they… they do nothing but make me sick to my heart.

KATE: I think you'd better leave now.

LORRAINE: (Offering his card.) If you have any questions, if there's anything I can do—

MOIRA snatches LORRAINE's card.

MOIRA: I expect to hear from you. I expect… I need to know where my husband… met his… end. I need some… semblance of … peace. So you make it soon. Preferably before I die.

LORRAINE: Mrs. Swanson—

MOIRA: Promises do not expire with the passage of time.

LORRAINE then MOIRA are gone, and—

Scene Three

It's October 23, 2017, and KATE is alone again in MOIRA's home with recorder, files and boxes. In her head she hears voices.

8 -YR-OLD MARY: Air Craft Flash.

MR. THORNE: Get off the line. We're in the middle of a conversation here.

MARY: Air Craft Flash.

MRS. WELLS: Is that you, Mary Browning?

MARY: I saw a jet, Mrs. Wells. It flew over like a silver streak. BOOM! I gotta report it. AIR CRAFT FLASH!

The sounds of a jet flying overhead, then—

Scene Four

The sound of the jet becomes the sound of laughter and a radio playing Johnny Mathis singing "It's Not for Me to Say." KATE steps into March 22, 1956 and their home in Married Quarters on the Comox Base. Young MOIRA sings and swings to the music with (or for) sixteen-month-old KATE, whose presence is created by MOIRA's mimed interactions with the child. Adult KATE responds verbally to her mum.

MOIRA: "It's not for me to say you love me"' Dee dum dee dum dee dum dee dum dee dum… This song sends me right over the moon and back again, kid… Mummy has landed. How about you make this cookie all by yourself?

KATE: Okay.

MOIRA: I'll just roll the dough up into a little ball and… ta da. Now it's over to you. No no, we don't eat it until it's baked and yummy. Take this fork and press down on the dough to make your peanie-butter cookie flat. / Gently!

KATE: Oops.

MOIRA: Never mind. Try again. That's my clever girl.

Knocking on door.

MOIRA: *(Calling.)* On my way. *(To Kate.)* I'll be right back. You stay put, baby.

MOIRA opens the door into Wind. FLYING OFFICER SCOTT — SCOTTY — stands on the stoop in dress uniform.

MOIRA: Holy smokes. Look at you, Scotty.

SCOTTY removes his cap.

MOIRA: Excuse the state of me. Katie and I are making peanut butter cookies. Come on in, get out of that wind. You can be our official cookie test— Oh!

SCOTTY: Moira?!

MOIRA: The baby. Pheeew. That was the doozy of all kicks.

SCOTTY: Let me help you.

MOIRA: I'm fine. Strong as a horse and stubborn as a mule. At least that's what Vic likes to tell me.

SCOTTY: You'd better sit down.

KATIE: *(Calling.)* Mum.

MOIRA: In a minute, Katie. (To Scotty.) No time for sitting. The kid and I are smack dab in the middle of it and I shudder to think what's happening in that kitchen right now. She'll be mighty happy to see her Uncle Scotty. Come on in. I'll make us a fresh pot of coffee.

She pulls him in and shuts the door.

SCOTTY: No coffee, thanks.

MOIRA: You're going to need an apron.

She sets off to get the apron.

MOIRA: I've got one with pink roses that would be lovely with your complexion.

SCOTTY: Not on your life.

MOIRA: I'll wear it then. You can wear mine. Actually, it's Vic's.

She takes her apron off as she speaks, ties it on SCOTTY.

MOIRA: He was supposed to be making these damn cookies. You know how he loves to bake. And eat. But Darryl James just kept after him. He didn't want to wait another whole day to qualify on those instruments. Of course, my Old Softy crumbles and… Scotty, what the hell is going on? Will you please just talk to me?

SCOTTY: Vic's plane. One moment… it was there. The next it disappeared. Over the Straight.

MOIRA: *(Beat.)* Vic's been in plenty of scrapes before. He always comes home. Best damn pilot on this base. Everyone says so.

SCOTTY: This comes straight from the horse's mouth. Felix Mackenzie.

MOIRA: What's Felix got to do with anything?

SCOTTY: Radar.

MOIRA: I'll get my coat.

KATE: *(Calling.)* Mum!

MOIRA: In a minute, Katie.

SCOTTY: Look, the best thing you can do right now is stay here, finish up the baking, then take a load off. Treat yourself to a rye and seven and a little lie-down.

KATIE: Mum?

MOIRA: A little lie-down?

KATIE Mum!

MOIRA: In a minute!

SCOTTY: What's most important right now is you and Katie and the baby.

MOIRA: *(Exiting.)* I'm pregnant, not made of glass.

SCOTTY: *(Calling after her.)* For Vic. Please. Our men are out there now. Searching. I promise you, everything possible is being done. We're going to find them—

MOIRA enters, now dressed for the weather and pushing a stroller.

MOIRA: Yes, we are.

MOIRA thrusts a cookie sheet into SCOTTY's hands, steps into the wind with "Toddler KATE" in stroller and pulls the door shut.

Scene Five

KATE joins MOIRA, who pushes the stroller into the wind and across the base. Trees snap back and forth, newspapers and candy bar wrappers fly past the window. Then a sock monkey rolls past.

MOIRA: Did you see that, baby? A sock monkey. It's rolling away. *(To sock monkey.)* Bye bye.

KATE: Bye bye.

COMMANDING OFFICER BUCKLES blows in, bringing his office with him.

BUCKLES: Moira.

MOIRA: Commander Buckles.

BUCKLES: Charlie, please. Hello, Katie. My goodness, how /you've grown.

MOIRA: Is there news? I mean, since I left Scotty, Lieutenant Scott—

BUCKLES: No, not a darn thing. Have a seat, dear.

MOIRA: I need to know everything.

BUCKLES: Of course you do. And Lieutenant Scott will have told you all there is to tell.

MOIRA: I won't rest until I know everything.

BUCKLES: The plane simply... disappeared. It's the darnedest thing. But rest assured, our men are out there searching. Round the clock.

MOIRA: Out where?

BUCKLES: They're over Georgia Straight near Quadra Island.

MOIRA: Was the plane spotted?

BUCKLES: No. There was a loud sound reported by fishermen in the area. A "boom," /and so…

MOIRA: An explosion?!

BUCKLES: It's probably nothing, might be some trouble at one of the mills up there. But, naturally, we're checking. Now you know as much as I do. And as soon as I learn anything new, I promise you'll be the first person I contact.

MOIRA: I'm going to hold you to that, sir.

BUCKLES: You must be tired. I'll have one of the men show you home.

MOIRA: I need to talk to Felix Mackenzie.

BUCKLES: I'm afraid he's gone for the day. /Moira?

MOIRA: *(Exiting.)* Thank you. I need to find Felix now.

As BUCKLES and KATE watch, MOIRA pushes the stroller off into the wind. Then it's—

Five days later. WIND, MOIRA, and KATIE enter COMMANDER BUCKLES' office.

BUCKLES: Hello. You girls are early today.

MOIRA: Surprise.

BUCKLES: I told Eva before I left the house that I was beginning to think I could set my watch around your afternoon visits.

MOIRA: What news?

BUCKLES: Nothing yet.

MOIRA: Help me.

BUCKLES: This weather's been a major hindrance. But you know what they say, dear. No news is—

MOIRA: I'm losing my mind.

BUCKLES: As soon as I know anything, you'll know. You have my word on that.

MOIRA: There must be someone you can speak to right now. While I'm here.

Someone you can phone. Someone who knows what the hell is going on.

BUCKLES: The search wheels are turning slowly and I understand it's painful, but I promise it's what you want.

MOIRA: Are you losing your mind?

BUCKLES: These men are professionals, dear. Colleagues. They're doing everything humanly possible. Risking their own lives.

MOIRA: There must be someone overseeing the search. Or someone who's out there on the water or in the air even now, looking for them. I know they have to report back. They contact you. They must. You're Vic's commanding officer. He has such respect for you.

BUCKLES: We need to be patient, Moira.

MOIRA: I need my husband. My child needs, our children need their daddy.

BUCKLES: You must understand that we're doing everything humanly possible. Oh dear, I'm sorry to run off, but I'm going to be late for a critical meeting with the—

MOIRA: Do I stink?

BUCKLES: I beg your pardon.

MOIRA: I know it's not Katie, so it must be me.

BUCKLES: I don't follow.

MOIRA: Is the stench of my need, my desperation, too awful to bear?

BUCKLES: What in the name of God—

MOIRA: How else do I explain the reception I receive from the fellas here? Every day this week, within minutes, no, seconds after we arrive in this office, Vic's friends and colleagues, my friends, Katie's "uncles," race to their desks to pick up their telephones and begin dialling furiously or they're off to "critical" meetings or they bury their heads in /files and ledgers.

BUCKLES: Moira, please, everyone in this community is bleeding for you and for Laura James and her children.

MOIRA: That must be painful for everyone in this community.

BUCKLES: You're not yourself.

MOIRA: I have never been more myself.

BUCKLES: My dear—

MOIRA: Is it true what they're saying? That Felix Mackenzie got up to stretch his long legs and turned around to find Vic's plane gone?

BUCKLES: Who's saying that?

MOIRA: Everyone on this base. When they think I'm out of earshot.

BUCKLES: Felix is a good man and a damn fine officer.

MOIRA: Felix is never here when I come calling. He's never in his quarters, never in the canteen or the mess. I must stink to high heavens.

Beat.

BUCKLES: Eva asked me to invite you girls over for dinner tonight. Nothing fancy, just a simple family meal. Wednesdays are roast chicken and Eva's famous baking powder biscuits and gravy.

MOIRA: The gals in Married Quarters have all been very kind.

BUCKLES: We're a community, Moira.

MOIRA: Doreen and Helen offered to take Katie off my hands for an hour, two, a whole day at a time. Did you know that? To give me a little peace. Peace? They mean well, but I'm not letting our baby girl out of my sight, not even for a minute. Phyllis and Merle and your Eva deliver casseroles, soups and fresh baked bread to our door. I could set up my own canteen and make a small fortune.

But Charlie, I cannot sit in their kitchens. I cannot watch their sweet husbands kiss them hello, play with their kids and then carve their chickens and load their… baking powder biscuits with gravy.

Beat.

BUCKLES: *(Calls.)* Lieutenant Mackenzie. You have a visitor.

Instantly, LIEUTENANT FELIX MACKENZIE appears. If actor playing BUCKLES is transforming to play FELIX, BUCKLES' next line and exit are cut.

BUCKLES: I'll leave you to it then.

BUCKLES exits.

FELIX: Moira.

MOIRA: Hello, Felix. Is it true?

FELIX: …

MOIRA: Felix.

FELIX: Did I get up, stretch and pour a quick coffee like I always do after a long haul on the job? You bet I did. It's procedure.

MOIRA: Procedure?

FELIX: Essential. Sit too long and my legs calcify. Arthritis. And my eyes, they burn—

MOIRA: Who watches the screen while you're up?

FELIX: Two, maybe three minutes tops my back was turned.

WIND begins to gust up.

FELIX: Look, they're going to find Vic and Darryl and bring them safely home. I believe that. I have to. You believe it, right? I need to know you… Moira?

MOIRA: Oh, I believe they're coming home all right, but if you're looking for absolution, look elsewhere.

FELIX watches MOIRA and KATE disappear. He's blown off the stage and—

Scene Six

Immediately, the sound of newborn STEVIE howling in their home in Married Quarters. (This sound can be made live by the actor playing STEVIE, or by a recording.) As KATE watches, MOIRA, in her nightgown, appears holding "Stevie" (a doll, a blanket wrapped to look like a baby, or just a mimed baby) and a drink and puffing on a cigarette. There's a knock on the door.

MOIRA: Oh shit. Not now.

More knocking. She puts "Stevie" down. "Stevie" cries and shrieks intermittently throughout the scene.

MOIRA: You can't go to the door looking like this. *(Searching.)* Sweater. You put it down here somewhere.

More knocking. MOIRA opens door to find SCOTTY. She tries to hide her face from him.

MOIRA: Scotty.

SCOTTY: Hello, Moira.

MOIRA: I thought you were Doc Leslie. He's taken to dropping in on us unexpectedly.

SCOTTY: Good man.

MOIRA: He's a snoop.

SCOTTY: Mind if I come in?

MOIRA: The doc keeps telling me I need to pull myself together. *(As Doc.)* "Moira, your temper, the outbursts, the state of your house, your personal hygiene, and, well, your children. Have you thought about spending some time in Winnipeg with your folks?"

SCOTTY: Hey, look at me. How are you doing?

MOIRA: Stevie's a difficult baby.

SCOTTY: I'd sure love to meet him.

MOIRA: Colicky.

SCOTTY: Stand still for a minute, would you? I can't see you.

MOIRA: Please don't.

SCOTTY: Is that blood on your face?

MOIRA: I said don't.

SCOTTY: Moira, this is Scotty you're talking to. Look at me.

She does.

MOIRA: Boils. On my face, my neck, my arms, my stomach… Head to toe. Our son was born covered in them. And my hair, my lovely hair, it's coming out in clumps, Scotty. In my comb, my brush, Stevie's little fists. Doc Leslie says it's the shock.

SCOTTY: Hey, hey, come here.

A hug.

SCOTTY: I'm so sorry. For everything that's happening.

MOIRA: Oh, it feels good to be held. I'd forgotten. How good, how good.

Kate (Terry Lynn Boyle) conjures up Moira (Clarice McCord) in Married Quarters on Comox Air Base in 1956, introducing newborn Stevie to Scotty (Darrian Gaetz).

MOIRA steps out of the hug.

MOIRA: Will you come in if I promise to behave like a civilized human being?

SCOTTY: I'd like that.

They're in the house and there's a big STEVIE squall.

MOIRA: I don't think he ever sleeps. It's like this all the time. Let me introduce you properly.

MOIRA fetches "Stevie."

MOIRA: Stephen Victor Swanson, I want you to meet your Uncle Scotty. Jonathan Gordon Scott. Your daddy's best friend.

SCOTTY takes "Stevie" in his arms.

SCOTTY: Hey there, little fella.

MOIRA: Careful. His skin.

SCOTTY: Poor kid.

STEVIE stops squalling.

MOIRA: I think he likes you.

SCOTTY: Damn right he likes me. Wow. You're the spitting image of your dad, Stephen.

MOIRA: He has Vic's face. *(Beat.)* Let me get you some coffee. Or a drink if you'd like. I've got rye and ginger.

SCOTTY: I'd love to, but—

MOIRA: Live a little. How about a G & T?

SCOTTY: I'm working today.

MOIRA: All right, but if you change your mind—

SCOTTY: Moira, just sit down for a minute. Please.

MOIRA: I'm so jumpy these days. And I haven't spent real time with anyone over the age of sixteen months since Vic…

SCOTTY: That can't be good for you.

MOIRA: I don't want any more pity visits. Pastor Warren was here earlier.

SCOTTY: The pastor means well, Moira.

MOIRA: He pushed a bouquet of waxy white lilies into my arms and invited me to join his congregation in prayer.

SCOTTY: Oh, Jesus—

MOIRA: Exactly. He says the kids and I should thank Christ that Vic has gone to a better place. What gives that supercilious little rodent the right? Vic is in hell.

SCOTTY: /No, Moira.

MOIRA: He's lost and afraid, or he may be wandering somewhere with amnesia, but he's alive. I know this, Scotty. Vic /is alive.

SCOTTY: Hey, hey, shh. I'm with you all the way… You didn't murder Pastor Warren, did you?

MOIRA: I threw him out the door. Then I tossed those dead-faced lilies after him and watched the wind carry the whole damn mess away.

SCOTTY: Listen, I was thinking… maybe Doc Leslie's onto something. Maybe you should consider going to Winnipeg.

MOIRA: …

SCOTTY: Your mum and dad must be worried sick about you.

MOIRA: I'm not going to Winnipeg.

SCOTTY: A visit would do you and the kids the world of good. Escape from this place. Let your mum and dad take care of you.

MOIRA: Vic takes care of me.

SCOTTY: He'd hate that you're alone.

MOIRA: I'm not alone. And he'll be home soon.

SCOTTY: Oh shit… Moira… Look… We're able to give you one more month.

MOIRA: One month?

SCOTTY: You knew this was coming.

MOIRA: Are you evicting Laura James and her kids, too?

SCOTTY: There's a waiting list for Married Quarters. We have two families ready to move in.

MOIRA: I can't speak for Laura, but at least one of those families is just going to have to keep on waiting.

SCOTTY: Please don't make this more difficult than it /already is.

MOIRA: No, you don't. You don't, you don't get to throw us out of our home and paint me the villain. You get to find Vic and Darryl James. That's what you get to do. Go on. Do it. Get to work. Now. Do it.

SCOTTY: The fellas have taken up a collection. I know I speak for all of them when I say—

MOIRA: Put that away!

SCOTTY: We wish it could be more.

MOIRA: I don't want your goddamn money! You're going to have to carry us out of our home. You hear that? You tell that to the fellas. We're staying right here until Vic comes home. Flying Officer Victor Swanson. Your colleague, your best friend, my husband, the father of these two children, he's coming home.

SCOTTY: Forgive me.

MOIRA shuts the door. Transition into driving snow in—

Scene Seven

Winnipeg. Evening. MOIRA in her nightgown stands at a window watching the storm in progress. Sounds of colicky STEVIE. KATE is watching.

MOIRA: Oh, Winnipeg. I'd almost forgotten.

She picks up an official-looking envelope, then puts it back down. KATE has that same envelope in her hands.

MOIRA: Coward.

MOIRA rips the envelope open and reads to herself. Concurrently, KATE pulls the letter out of the previously opened envelope and reads it aloud.

KATE: November 15, 1956

Dear Mrs. Swanson,

It is with deep regret that I must advise you that your husband, Flying Officer Victor Stephen Swanson, is now for official purposes presumed to have died on March 22nd, 1956, and I wish to offer you and your family my sincere and heartfelt sympathy.

It is my earnest hope, however, that you will find comfort in the knowledge of your husband's contribution to his Country both during and subsequent to the Second World War.

Yours sincerely—

MOIRA drops the letter and returns to the window. A figure takes shape in the dark. A man… a pilot… a ghost.

MOIRA: You're here. Here. Vic!

She opens the door and exits the house. Through the window KATE watches her mother race into the weather which swallows VIC first and then MOIRA.

Scene Eight

And it's October 23, 2017. KATE is back in the house, alone with the boxes, files and recorder. Again, she hears MARY's voice.

YOUNG MARY'S VOICE: Aircraft flash!

KATE: Mary is in her seventies now. She's the mother of one of my ex-students. The two of you actually met at one of our theatre productions. Growing up, Mary lived on an acreage north of Pemberton. The way she remembers it, the adult world then was settling into—

MARY begins speaking.

OLD MARY'S VOICE: a bad case of paranoia — the Cold War — and because of our location in the coastal mountain area, my family is selected to watch for aircraft and report immediately: the type, direction and time spotted.

This day I spot a jet, run to the house and pick up the phone. We're on a party line from Squamish to Bridge River. There are two people talking. As instructed, I say "Air Craft Flash." I say it three times, but the old farts won't get off the line. It takes me maybe two hours to finally report that sighting. By that time a jet that fast could be, oh … who knows?

The sound of a jet plane overhead becomes a loud recording of one of the songs MOIRA and VIC once called their own.

Scene Nine

And it's October 4, 2016. We're in ninety-year-old MOIRA's home. KATE watches her mum who, lost in the music, dances.

KATE: Mum.

No response. STEVIE, unseen and unheard by MOIRA, materializes. As KATE watches he raises a paper bag to his mouth and inhales.

KATE: No! /Stop!

KATE's "Stop!" overlaps with STEVIE popping the bag and disappearing.

KATE: Shit!

MOIRA: I hope you did. In your pants. Serve you right for sneaking up on an old woman. You're lucky I didn't drop down dead.

KATE: God, I wish you'd wear your hearing aid.

MOIRA: I do as I like.

KATE: Ain't that the truth.

MOIRA: And I don't like spies.

KATE: I wasn't spying.

MOIRA: That was private.

KATE: I'm sorry.

MOIRA: I must have looked ridiculous.

KATE: Beautiful.

MOIRA: Time to get your eyes examined, kid. I'm eighty-six years old and the shaking isn't rehearsed.

KATE: You're ninety years old.

MOIRA: Am I really?

KATE: 'Fraid so.

MOIRA: Your Mountie called this morning.

KATE: Sergeant Bradley phoned here?

MOIRA: They're going out again.

KATE: When?

MOIRA: Saturday after next. A big group. That search and rescue fella up there at the motel—

KATE: His name is Chris Seers. And it's the Callaghan Mountain Lodge.

MOIRA: I'm going with them.

KATE: Over my dead body.

MOIRA: That can be arranged.

KATE: There's no way they're going to take you on a search and rescue mission.

MOIRA: I'm going with my daughter.

KATE: Not a chance.

MOIRA: Your attendance is required. Sergeant *(Groping for name.)* Mountie wants your fingerprints. And a sample of your blood.

KATE: My blood?

MOIRA: For something called… *(Searching.)* DNA.

KATE: That makes sense.

MOIRA: Does it?

KATE: My DNA would be a match for Dad's. Like in all those murder mysteries you watch. So, if they do find… anything, and they've got my fingerprints and blood, which will give them my DNA, they should be able to tell if it's… him.

MOIRA: Vic's body?

KATE: There won't be a body, not after all this time. Teeth maybe.

MOIRA begins to gulp for air.

KATE: Mum? Let your breath out before you breathe in. Slowly, remember how the nurse showed us?

MOIRA: No!

KATE: Like this. Watch me. Good. You can breathe in now, not big gulps, not yet, just little tiny sips of air.

MOIRA does as she's instructed and keeps it up.

KATE: It's probably gonna snow anyway. And if it snows, they'll cancel the search again. But, if the weather holds, I promise I'll go up there to deliver my DNA to Sergeant Bradley.

MOIRA: We're going together.

KATE: You'd last one second out there.

MOIRA: How little you know me.

KATE: You don't even go outside the house without your walker. I won't take you.

MOIRA: I'll catch a bus.

KATE: And then what? Are you going to hike in?

MOIRA: If I have to.

KATE: There are no benches along the way and no Starbucks around the corner.

MOIRA: Patronizing, patronizing, patronizing.

KATE: We're talking forest, temperatures way below zero.

MOIRA: I can take it. I can take anything. I grew up in Winnipeg.

KATE: Mountains. Grizzly bears.

MOIRA: Oh lord…

KATE: The place is riddled with them.

MOIRA: The bears will be sleeping.

KATE: Wow, who knew you were an expert on the hibernation routines of grizzly bears. Mum, you're driving me out of my fucking mind.

MOIRA: Then "fucking" help me. He's up there.

KATE: Even ten years ago you might have—

MOIRA: He. Is. Up. There.

KATE: You might have been able to—

MOIRA: This is my last chance. I will not let you shove me to the side like some dribbling child.

KATE: Then stop behaving like one.

MOIRA lunges at KATE to slap her, loses her balance. KATE reaches to help, but MOIRA avoids her and manages to stop herself from falling.

MOIRA: Damn you! I'm the woman who gave you life, who wiped your shitty little behind, who slaved for years as a lowly stenographer for the money to feed and clothe you.

KATE: You go after me like that again and I'm leaving this house and never coming back.

Beat.

MOIRA: Promise me you'll take me up to find Vic.

KATE: I don't know what to say, Mother.

MOIRA: You say yes, Daughter.

Beat.

MOIRA: Please.

KATE: I'll do my best to find him.

MOIRA: And you will /take

KATE: I will not take you up that mountain.

Scene Ten

It's October 23, 2017, and KATE is alone again in MOIRA's home with files and boxes.

KATE: It's early morning a little over a year ago. *(Referring to a tiny notebook.)* Saturday, October 14th, 2016. I'm at Base Camp in the Callaghan Valley.

CHRIS SEERS materializes at Base Camp partway through his address to search and rescue volunteers. KATE is there, too, listening.

CHRIS: This may be "cold case meets search and rescue, "but your responsibility to our pilots is as real today, in October 2016, as it would have been in 1956 if there'd been a call to action then. We will solve this mystery, if not this year, then the next or the next or the next… you get the picture. I hope you're all in good form today. When your leg muscles start screaming, think of our pilots. It was March when they were up here. Snow would have been drifting up to their armpits.

Refers to map to review procedure.

One more time: In your teams of three you'll work your way up your designated corridors. The compass bearer in each team will head up the middle of your corridor, keeping you on course. Searchers meanwhile criss-cross horizontally as the three of you climb to the top. You will then move one corridor to the east and repeat the process as you head back down to Base Camp and a hot meal. Any questions? …Going, going, going, gone. See you on the chow side.

CHRIS begins to go.

KATE: *(Calling.)* Chris.

CHRIS: Hey. Kate, right?

KATE: "Our pilots"? When the hell did you and your posse take ownership of my dad and Darryl James?

CHRIS: Is there /a problem?

KATE: Do you ever think about the people left behind? The ones who loved "your" pilots? Still love them and /grieve them?

CHRIS: Can we talk later? /I'm kind of busy here.

KATE: They were husbands, fathers, sons, brothers, friends. Who the fuck are you in this equation?

CHRIS: I'm the one who's gonna solve this mystery.

KATE: Wow. Will that be today?

CHRIS: Maybe. I'd like that. Wouldn't you?

KATE: You're out of your mind. Look /around you.

CHRIS: Takes one to know one.

KATE: We're talking about my father here. What's your excuse?

CHRIS: Seriously?

KATE: Yup.

CHRIS: This one just reached out and yanked me by the balls.

KATE: Ouch. /Poor you.

CHRIS: And I guess I figured those people you're talking about, the ones who lost their fathers and husbands and friends might find some peace in knowing where and /how and

KATE: Oh shit, forget it. I'm sorry. It's just… it's terrifying being up here, so close to where they… *(Beat.)* Do you really believe it's possible that my dad and Darryl James survived the crash? That they were alive up here?

CHRIS: I do. God knows why.

KATE: What's that supposed to mean?

CHRIS: The ejection seats on the T-33s were famous for…

KATE: Say it.

CHRIS: Neck-snapping. And if our pilots survived the ejection with their … heads intact, most probable scenario? A tree or two snagged their chutes on the way down, and they died… up there. But if they beat the odds, and I believe they did, the proof is here. Look, I found something years ago, then, like a fool, I forgot all about it. Until I met Archie, he's the hiker who found the jet's canopy back in 1974.

KATE: I'd love to shake that man's hand.

CHRIS: Then you will.

SEARCHER OS: *(Calling.)* Chris! Let's /go.

CHRIS: Two minutes. *(To KATE.)* Years ago, Archie and me are having a couple of beers, and he starts telling me about the mystery of the 'disappeared' pilots. That's when it all comes screaming back. *(Remembering.)* I was hiking alone that day.

KATE: That's crazy-ass stupid.

CHRIS: Pushing my crazy ass through wind and thick brush, and I stumble on the remains of this old campfire. Logs shoved together to make a seating area. Empty sardine cans, two metal cups, two spoons, two knives, weathered, like something displayed in a museum. Still, I didn't think too much about it at the time. Just some hikers or maybe prospectors, couldn't be bothered to pack their supplies out.

KATE: But…?

CHRIS: Parachute cord. Reams of the stuff. I did some research. Sure enough, those were the kinds of emergency supplies … our pilots … would have been packing.

KATE: Take me to this place. Please.

CHRIS: Yeah, it's just, I can't exactly remember where it is.

KATE: Are you fucking kidding me?

CHRIS: I know, I know. Look, Kate, every year we're narrowing the parameters of this search. When I find that campsite, and I'm gonna find that campsite, we're on the homestretch.

Scene Eleven

It's October 5, 2016, MOIRA's home. KATE is going through files MOIRA gave her. From another area, the sound of a blaring television: Wheel of Fortune. *Television light reveals MOIRA, wearing a new pair of hiking boots, watching the show.*

MOIRA: *(Answering game show question.)* A bird in the hand!

TV goes to commercial break and is even louder.

KATE: *(Calling.)* Turn it down! I'm trying to read these files.

KATE is now with MOIRA.

KATE: Could you at least mute the damn commercials?

Commercials are muted.

MOIRA: Did you want something?

KATE: Thank you.

MOIRA: How old would that Vanna creature be now?

KATE: Beats me. Late sixties?

MOIRA: Must be made of plastic.

KATE: Are you ever going to take those boots off?

MOIRA: I'm breaking them in for our trip.

KATE: Oh, are you going somewhere?

MOIRA: Fifty percent off. Fifty percent. Comfortable, too. My corns are talking to me, but they're not screaming.

KATE: Yet.

MOIRA: I recommend you get yourself down to Capitol Iron first thing tomorrow. Last day of the sale. Remarkable deals on all the hiking gear. Did I show you the jacket and pants I bought?

KATE: Twice.

MOIRA: Oh, Plastic Woman and her Little Wheelie Man are back.

TV volume back on and MOIRA is lost in the television light and sound.

KATE with the files, picks out an old envelope. It's covered in psychedelic pencil crayon drawings and sealed. She opens it and out fall a couple of ancient joints.

Scene Twelve

MOIRA remains vaguely visible in TV screen light as fourteen-year-old STEVIE appears, barefoot, pants rolled up above his knees and smoking a joint. He brings a starry night and an ocean beach with him.

STEVIE: *(Announcing his presence.)* Uh eee uh uh eee uh eee. Uh eee uh uh eee uh. Over here!

KATE: Mum's gonna kill you.

STEVIE: The water's not even up to my knees.

KATE: It's October.

STEVIE: Candyass.

KATE: At least I'm not an idiot.

STEVIE: You sure about that, Candyass? Cuz it looks to me like I got the joint. *(Tokes.)* Great shit.

KATE: Give it to me.

STEVIE: Come and get it, Candyass.

KATE moves into the water.

KATE: Shitshitshitshitshit! Freezing!

KATE reaches for the joint.

STEVIE: Magic word.

KATE: Toke. Please… Hand it over!

STEVIE: First you gotta gimme Mum imitation #3: Hair in curlers, she wings the front door open when you show up pissed as a rat at two in the morning.

KATE: *(As MOIRA.)* "You miserable little bugger! Get in here!"

STEVIE: Bitchin'! You got the deranged eyeballs and clenched teeth down, baby.

They pass the joint, look at the stars.

KATE: Look. Orion.

STEVIE: Orion?

KATE: Shaped like a hunter. Or a warrior. Right there. See?

STEVIE: I don't see no warrior star.

KATE: It's a constellation. A whole bunch of connect-the-dot stars. The ancient Greeks named it Orion after a great hunter.

STEVIE: I still don't see it.

KATE: Follow my hand. Orion's belt. It starts down here and moves up like this. Got it?

STEVIE: Uh… yes!

KATE: Those are his shoulders and—

STEVIE: Our man's got a sword and a shield, baby. Far fucking out!

KATE: I like to imagine Orion moving.

STEVIE: Like flying?

KATE: Like those stone statues in cartoons that come alive. "Orion leaps across the universe in a single bound, battles with a massive, snorting bull and triumphs."

STEVIE: Lose the bull. What kind of warrior fights a man-cow?

A starry night on a Victoria ocean beach. Kate (Terry Lynn Boyle) introduces fourteen-year-old brother, Stevie (Darrian Gaetz), to the constellation of Orion.

KATE: Greek myths are loaded with man-cows. They hang out in mazes where they sacrifice virgins or they're really Zeus-in-Disguise. Zeus is always screwing some poor, helpless virgin.

STEVIE: Go, Zeus! Where'd you learn this stuff?

KATE: Mum.

STEVIE: No way.

KATE — only KATE — sees MOIRA in her dim TV screen reality.

KATE: We were right here. It was a night like this. She packed a thermos of hot chocolate and took us star watching.

STEVIE: Me, too?

KATE: No, we chained you to the rack in the basement and came by ourselves. Of course you, too.

STEVIE: Cool.

KATE: We were just little kids, eh. And she definitely skipped the Zeus-humping-helpless-Virgin story, but she's the one who introduced us to "The Great Warrior in the Sky."

STEVIE: I think… Yeah. Okay, this is kinda fucked up, but I kinda think I thought—

KATE: Think I thought?

STEVIE: I kinda think I thought Mum was talking about Dad. I mean I think I thought he was the great warrior in the sky.

KATE: I love that. I bet she was talking about Dad.

STEVIE: Yeah?

KATE: I love that.

STEVIE: *(Introducing great hero.)* Victor: Star Warrior.

KATE: Faster than a speeding meteor.

STEVIE: Able to leap and stab tall man-cows in a single bound.

KATE & STEVIE: Victor: Star Warrior!

STEVIE: Far out.

KATE: Do you think she ever went out with anyone, I mean after Dad disappeared?

STEVIE: You mean like was she balling some guy? Eeew, shit, I /hope not.

KATE: Grow up. Do you wish he was alive?

STEVIE: Yeah. You?

KATE: I honestly don't think I know anymore.

STEVIE: How come?

KATE: Everything would be different. Our friends… And Mum and Dad wanted four kids. We'd be living on an Air Force Base somewhere.

STEVIE: Fuck me. No, thanks. I wish I knew him, though. I wish Mum could be happy. Maybe she'd stop trying to kick my ass all the time.

KATE watches as MOIRA disappears.

KATE: *(To STEVIE.)* Do you believe in ghosts?

STEVIE: Not really, it kinda feels too easy, you know? Like heaven. I think… nah. I probably don't believe in reincarnation either, but it's crazy-cool.

KATE: Yeah.

STEVIE: I wouldn't wanna come back as someone else. I'd wanna come back as something else. Something better. Pure, you know? Something that doesn't fuck up everything he touches. /Maybe a bird.

KATE: Hey, stop it—

STEVIE: Yeah. A great blue heron. They are the coolest of the cool.

KATE: Oh, come on. They must be the world's loneliest birds.

STEVIE: Not at mating time, baby.

STEVIE pulls out a pack of cigarettes containing several joints, lights up, tokes.

STEVIE: *(Passing joint.)* Here.

KATE: Have you got hash in there, too?

STEVIE: Black Lebanese.

KATE: Where'd you get all the money?

STEVIE: You want this or not?

KATE: Please tell me you didn't steal it out of Mum's purse.

STEVIE: Fuck off.

KATE: I really can't go through that shit again.

STEVIE: I didn't take her money.

KATE: So how'd you pay for it?

STEVIE: I got it from Danny.

KATE: Are you crazy? The police are watching him all the time.

STEVIE: The fuzz are a pack of hairy assholes.

KATE: That doesn't change / anything.

STEVIE: Danny's cool. Don't sweat it. I'll pay him back.

KATE: Swear you didn't go into Mum's purse again.

STEVIE: This is bullshit.

KATE: Swear!

Beat. She grabs her shoes and stuff and begins to exit.

KATE: You're the real asshole!

STEVIE: Katie, wait! I swear.

KATE: I wanna believe you.

STEVIE: So do.

KATE: You'll regret it if you're lying to me.

STEVIE: I'm not lying.

KATE: I mean it.

STEVIE: I know.

KATE: …

STEVIE: Hey… I kinda hate to say this, but you know who you looked like just then? Mum #3. *(Imitating.)* "You're the real asshole! "

KATE: ...

STEVIE: *(About a foot race on the beach.)* Ready to be destroyed?

KATE: ...

STEVIE: Will you stop with the silent treatment?

KATE: ...

STEVIE: First one makes it to the steps and back here again wins. Ready?

KATE: ...

STEVIE: Ready?

KATE: I guess.

STEVIE: Read/y, set,

KATE: Go!

STEVIE: Hey!

KATE takes off first, STEVIE chases. There is laughter and screaming. Then STEVIE is gone.

Scene Thirteen

And KATE is with ninety-year-old MOIRA who sits on the beach wearing her new hiking boots and jacket. KATE has a thermos.

KATE: Warm enough?

MOIRA: Like toast. This new jacket is a marvel.

KATE: And such a deal. I made us some hot chocolate.

KATE pours.

MOIRA: *(Remembering.)* That's my job.

KATE: The stars are out in force, baby.

MOIRA: Baby?

KATE: A little blast from the past.

KATE points at Orion.

KATE: Follow my arm my hand my index finger up up up.

MOIRA: There. He's there! Star Warrior.

VIC appears. MOIRA tracks him.

KATE: I think Stevie thought you were talking about Dad when you told us about the Star Warrior.

MOIRA: Clever boy.

STEVIE'S VOICE ONLY: Uh eee uh uh eee uh eee.
Uh eee uh uh eee uh.

KATE: I feel like, like if I turn around quickly I'll find Stevie, but always just slightly out of reach, maybe log rolling or balancing on the edge of the roof or flying through the air. There are times I'd swear I can hear him. Crazy.

MOIRA: Uh eee uh uh eee uh.

KATE: How the hell did you /know.

MOIRA: That little theme song of his was crazy-making. But hearing him, that's not crazy. That's love.

KATE: Or guilt.

MOIRA: That's your Irish talking. Send it packing.

KATE: We never speak about him.

MOIRA: You have the photos now.

KATE: I found a couple from his sixteenth birthday.

MOIRA: Let's not spoil our night.

KATE: We dance around him.

MOIRA: So still. Not a breath of wind.

KATE: You were in the kitchen when I got home.

MOIRA: I'm not going back there, kid. It's too hard on my old heart.

KATE: You're always "back there" for Dad.

MOIRA: Vic is my heart.

KATE: Doesn't Stevie rate at least a valve or two?

MOIRA: What a ridiculous question.

KATE: Is it? Is it really?

MOIRA: My son's in *(Gestures to her heart.)* here all right, you better believe it.

Scene Fourteen

And it's STEVIE's sixteenth birthday. KATE joins YOUNG MOIRA — mid-forties — in the family home. STEVIE makes a big entrance, wearing shades.

STEVIE: Heeeeeeeeeeeere's Stevie!

MOIRA: Where's my birthday hug?

KATE with lit birthday cake begins to sing. Young MOIRA joins in, but probably with the original words. KATE's having fun with the song. She's also trying to warn STEVIE to wash up, get the smell off.

KATE: Happy birthday to you,
You were born in a zoo,
You look like a monkey
You smell like one too!

STEVIE: *(Like a Tarzan call.)* Uh eee uh eee uh eee uh eee uh!

KATE: You stink, little brother. Do us all a favour and /have a wash.

MOIRA: Katie, would you lay off, please?

STEVIE: Yeah, baby.

MOIRA: It's his birthday.

STEVIE: Oh yeah, baby.

MOIRA: You: make a wish.

STEVIE prepares to blow out candles.

MOIRA: Wait. Stop. Stop!

STEVIE: Jeez, Ma, make up your mind.

MOIRA: Take the sunglasses off. I want to see your face. Grandma and Grandpa will want to see that face.

KATE: Why?

STEVIE: Cuz they looove it.

MOIRA: Will you just get over there with your brother please? Give him a nice big hug, the way you used to.

KATE: My brother used to be cute and kinda huggable.

STEVIE: Hey! She said a hug, not a headlock!

KATE: …

STEVIE: Awww… Katie wuvs me, Mummy.

MOIRA: Glasses off.

STEVIE: Here's the deal. You take one pic with shades on, then one with shades off. We'll all wanna look back and remember how terminally cool I was on this day.

MOIRA scoops his sunglasses.

STEVIE: Hey! Gimme!

MOIRA: Say cheeeeesewhiz.

STEVIE: /Cheeeeesewhizontoastisbetterthanmost.

KATE: Cheeeeesewhizontoastisbetterthanmost.

MOIRA takes candle-blowing photo.

MOIRA: Now one with me.

MOIRA gives KATE the camera. She takes the picture, then STEVIE grabs his shades back and puts them on.

STEVIE: This is the life, eh? Chocolate cake with cocoa-butter icing and Smarties on top.

MOIRA: Katie, get the ice cream. And presents.

KATE: But—

MOIRA: Now. On the counter.

KATE exits.

MOIRA: Glue?

STEVIE: Scissors?

MOIRA: Don't give me lip, mister. Take the glasses off, look at me, and tell me you weren't sniffing glue.

STEVIE takes the glasses off.

MOIRA: You stupid child.

STEVIE: I wasn't sniffing glue.

MOIRA: Tell me another one. You reek.

STEVIE: Let go of me.

Enter KATE.

KATE: It's Brut.

STEVIE: Aftershave for Real Men, baby.

MOIRA: Don't you "baby" me.

KATE: They send samples in the mail.

MOIRA: How stupid do you think I am?

STEVIE: I haven't sniffed glue since I was, what, twelve?

MOIRA: I really don't know. But that first time is burned into my brain, mister. My little boy with his nose in a paper bag stepping off the roof and falling through the sky.

STEVIE: Me and Kate just had a few beers.

MOIRA: Uh uh. Hand it over.

STEVIE: What are you talking about?

MOIRA: The glue or whatever drug you've been poisoning yourself with this time.

STEVIE: There's nothing to hand over.

MOIRA: Why the hell should I believe one word you say?

STEVIE: Because it's the truth.

MOIRA: I don't think I've heard the truth out of you in at least six years.

STEVIE: I didn't sniff glue.

MOIRA: Nothing but lies and stealing and drugs and booze and more lies / and more stealing and more lies!

STEVIE: I'm not fucking lying!

KATE: Stop it!

MOIRA: When did you become a good for nothing / monster?

STEVIE: Fuck you!

KATE: Stop it, both of you!

Beat.

MOIRA: I don't know what to do with you anymore, Stephen. How to deal with any of this. Can we not, just once once once have a nice, normal family day? A happy goddamn birthday? Without me thinking you're going to throw yourself off the roof or overdose on pills or be tossed into a paddy wagon pissed drunk?

STEVIE: Don't cry, Mum. Please.

MOIRA: And you, young lady, I expect more /from you.

STEVIE: It's not her fucking fault.

MOIRA: Watch your goddamn mouth.

STEVIE: It was just a few beers, eh. For my sixteenth. My idea. My fault. Katie didn't even really want to.

MOIRA: I don't know how to do this.

KATE: You are doing it.

MOIRA: You need a father.

STEVIE: Fuck that shit again. *(Hands to ears.)* /Aaaaaa aaaaaaaaaaaaaaaaaaaaaaaaaaaa...

STEVIE carries on with this drowning-out-noise until KATE tells him to shut up.

KATE: He's fine. We're both fine.

MOIRA: He is not fine. He needs a father. You need a father.

KATE: Stevie, shut up! Mum, Mummy, please, just sit down. And give me the knife. I'll cut the cake.

STEVIE: It's my birthday. My cake. Hand it over. You wanna piece, Mum?

No reaction from MOIRA.

STEVIE: Mum?

Still no reaction from MOIRA.

KATE: Yeah, she does. Me, too.

STEVIE cuts cake. Gives himself a massive piece with ice cream and wolfs it down.

STEVIE: This is the best, the best cake I ever ate.

Beat.

STEVIE: I could eat the whole thing.

They eat in silence. KATE picks up the gifts and passes MOIRA the second package.

KATE: Mum?

MOIRA: Happy sweet sixteen.

KATE: From both of us.

STEVIE: No way… You didn't… Holy shit.

STEVIE tears the paper off. Inside each is a drum stick.

STEVIE: Holy shit! This is… Thank you. I… Holy shit! I love you, Ma.

MOIRA: I know, baby.

STEVIE: *(Hugging her.)* Katie!

KATE: You're crushing my head.

STEVIE: You're looking at the next John Bonham.

MOIRA: Who?

STEVIE: Shitkickingest drummer ever.

KATE: *(To MOIRA.)* Led Zeppelin.

STEVIE: Where's the kit?

MOIRA: Basement. Ed and Doreen were here earlier, and Ed set them up.

STEVIE takes off.

MOIRA: I want you to call Ed and say thanks. Did you hear me?

STEVIE: Call Ed!

MOIRA: And say thank you.

The sound of loud drumming, then it fades and—

Scene Fifteen

It is October 2017 again. KATE, alone with the files and boxes.

KATE: I'm nineteen. I wake up to the sound of screaming. Another nightmare. My dad lost and alone, somewhere in a coastal forest. I don't believe he can hear you calling, but I can't shut you out. I creep down the stairs and into the dark kitchen. There you are. Your long legs and bare feet moving, moving, always moving.

Immediately it's 1971. Young MOIRA — mid forties — appears sleepwalking. She wears a knee-length flannel nightgown — no holes, no bloodstains. Her legs and feet are bare. WIND howls, trees creak and the harness swings from a branch.

MOIRA: *(To "searchers.")* Get over here! I can't do everything by myself! Vic?

Seventeen-year-old STEVIE enters in his pyjamas carrying a blanket.

STEVIE: Help's on the way.

KATE: Shhh. No.

MOIRA: *(To STEVIE searcher.)* He's over here!

KATE: *(To STEVIE.)* We can't wake her up, it's not safe—

MOIRA: *(To VIC.)* They're coming, / my love.

KATE: She could have a heart attack or a stroke, maybe die—

STEVIE: *(To KATE.)* Hey, trust me. Done this before.

KATE: When?

MOIRA: Can you hear me, Vic?

STEVIE: Last time? The night you slept over at Brenda's so you could study for some "big mid-term exam." Or was that Neil's house?

KATE: /Shhh.

STEVIE: *(To MOIRA.)* Which tree?

MOIRA: There. The bottoms of his legs, his boots, do you see them?

STEVIE: Ahhh, sure.

MOIRA: He's not answering me. It's this icy bugger of a wind. It's done his ears in. Or maybe amnesia. He's been up here so long.

STEVIE: Hang onto this blanket for me, will ya?

STEVIE gently lays blanket on MOIRA's shoulders and finally she slows down.

MOIRA: Oh… Thank you… You look so much like… Vic?

STEVIE: Going up that tree now. Wish me luck.

MOIRA: *(Awake, realizing.)* Stevie. What is going… where…?

And she realizes she's in the house.

STEVIE: Hiya, Ma.

MOIRA: Oh, I'm sorry, baby. Did I scare you?

STEVIE: Nah, but I'm pretty sure Katie crapped her drawers.

KATE: Stuff it.

MOIRA: What time is it?

KATE: 3:37.

MOIRA: In the morning?!

STEVIE: Yeah, baby.

MOIRA: Get back to your beds.

KATE: We'll go when you do.

MOIRA: You've got school in the morning.

STEVIE: You've got work in the morning.

MOIRA: Smartass kids.

STEVIE: Will you just keep that blanket on, please?

KATE: I'll get your slippers and bathrobe. *(To STEVIE.)* Maybe get Mum some herbal tea.

KATIE exits.

MOIRA: No tea.

STEVIE: Water?

MOIRA: Nope.

STEVIE: Gin then.

MOIRA Why not?

STEVIE pours her a glass of G & T and sneaks a few swigs straight from the bottle.

MOIRA: Nobody gives a damn.

STEVIE: Hey, screw that.

/KATIE enters.

MOIRA: I don't mean you kids.

KATE: *(About slippers.)* Put them on. And the robe.

MOIRA: Department of Defence bureaucrats, military, the lot. They blew this one big time.

KATE: We know.

MOIRA: So eager to bury your father and Darryl James in some filing vault in Ottawa so we'll just / forget and bugger off.

KATE: Stop it.

MOIRA: Vic calls to me—

STEVIE: No way, Ma.

MOIRA: Yes, way.

STEVIE: Okay, so Dad calls you in these nightmares from… a telephone booth?

MOIRA: You're a real scream, Stephen.

STEVIE: You told me he didn't even answer you.

MOIRA: When?

STEVIE: You said he couldn't hear, / something about the icy wind.

KATE: Stop this! Both of you! Dad's been gone more than seventeen years.

MOIRA: Seventeen, thirty-four, sixty-eight, it's irrelevant. Laugh if you like, kiddies, but your father's sending me messages… directions—

STEVIE: Okay, you're freaking me / out now.

MOIRA: These nightmares are more than by-products of my loneliness and grief, but I'm not completely crazy, I do know they're about that, too.

KATE: What's wrong with Stevie and me?

MOIRA: What are /you talking about?

STEVIE: Hey, Katie, not now—

KATE: Why are we never enough for you?

MOIRA: For god's sake, the two of you are my life, but your father, he's the reason we're here/ together now.

KATE: Half the reason.

MOIRA: My other half.

KATE: Your ghost.

MOIRA: Oh sweetie, I know this is hard on you kids, and I worry—

KATE: So let go. Even for just a day. Can you do that? Go one day without obsessing about him, without researching and plotting and sleepwalking—

MOIRA: I was not walking in my sleep.

STEVIE: Yes, you were.

KATE: Can you just try? Please. Wouldn't Dad want the three of us to be happy right /here, right now?

STEVIE: He'd want us to be sleeping.

Pause.

KATE: Mum?

MOIRA: I was just thinking of the day you were born.

KATE: What are you doing?

MOIRA: Your dad was in Ontario training to fly the, it was the CF 100 jet, when he got the news that I was in the hospital and, somehow or other, contacted his commanding officer. And damned if he didn't convince the man that he had to be in Winnipeg for your birth. A flight was arranged.

STEVIE: Just for Dad?

MOIRA: Yes.

STEVIE: Far out.

MOIRA: Yes. Your Uncle Gerry picked him up at the airport. They were at the hospital when you arrived, Kate. Your dad brought you a stuffed toy, it was bigger than you. A white bunny-rabbit. He said it was the happiest day of his life. And you better believe he was counting the days until he'd meet you, Stevie.

STEVIE: /Yeah?

KATE: *(Exiting.)* Good night.

MOIRA: Katie?

STEVIE: She's okay. She liked your story. 'Night, Ma.

MOIRA: 'Night, baby.

STEVIE exits. KATE comes back, unseen by MOIRA. MOIRA sees VIC or feels his presence.

MOIRA: /There you are.

KATE stops when MOIRA reaches out, in vain, for VIC. And a cold WIND takes us back to—

Scene Sixteen

Base Camp, Callaghan Valley, October 14, 2016 as before. KATE interviews/records CHRIS.

CHRIS: It's March 1997. Jack Perkes and I are doing some construction work in the Callaghan Lodge. We pack it in, hit the kitchen for dinner and a couple of beers. Then I head upstairs to lay my body down. In minutes I'm dozing off. It had been a long, hard day and we have another couple of the same coming up… I hear footsteps approaching on the stairs. Loud footsteps. I call out to Jack to keep it down. Nothing. More footsteps. Louder, closer, a kind of hollow sound, oddly metallic. I figure Jack's playing me, banging a length of pipe or something like that on the concrete to give me a scare. He's always been a bit of a prankster. I tell him to piss off. No reply, no laughter. Now that worries me some because Jack's a laugher. An exploder. He cannot hold it in… I sit up and there's someone square in the middle of the doorway. A man. Not Jack. This man is nowhere near as tall or heavy as Jack and he's dressed like a pilot. Helmet, boots, pack, the works. But everything's a little off. I call out, "Who's there?" Nothing. Just this silent man in the doorway. I can't see a face and, I won't lie, I wonder if he even has one. Then he turns and disappears… I stay right the hell where I am.

The next morning, we get sunshine. And over a strong cup of coffee and a plate of ham and eggs, I decide it must have been Jack all along. I'm gonna call him on it when he joins me, but the first thing he asks me is what the hell I thought I was getting up to in the night. Damned if he didn't hear the footsteps and see that man at his door. So I ask him, what did you see? Be specific. How tall? Describe the uniform. What kind of helmet?

What we saw was not a man. What we saw was an apparition.

KATE: No.

CHRIS: I know what you're thinking, but remember, it was the anniversary of their disappearance. March 22nd… Did I forget to say that?

KATE: Yup.

CHRIS: The uniform was vintage '50s. And there have been more sightings. Lodge staff, guests. You can ask anyone up here. Always at night. Always in and around the Lodge. It's one of our lost pilots. Kate? Are you okay?

KATE: Should I be?

Scene Seventeen

And KATE is again in MOIRA's home in October 2017 with the files and memories. As she speaks, MOIRA appears and acts out those directions.

KATE: You're in your late sixties now. Clutching a letter, you open the window, and—

MOIRA breathes deeply as WIND rushes in, then screams.

MOIRA: Aaaaaah!

And KATE's with her.

KATE: Mum?

MOIRA: My head is going to explode.

KATE: It's freezing in here.

KATE moves to shut the window or door.

MOIRA: Don't! I can't breathe.

KATE: Okay. Maybe sit down? Maybe not. What is that?

MOIRA: A reply from the Honourable Alison Cooper to my inquiry about the plane's canopy. I sent that letter over four months ago. July 21st, 1991.

KATE: And Alison Cooper is…?

MOIRA: The Associate Minister of National Defence.

KATE: That's good. Isn't it?

MOIRA: *(Reading.)* "No further information than what you already have on the recovered canopy frame is available."

KATE: Oh. So… this is the end of it then?

MOIRA: No, Kate, this is not the end of it because obviously this "honourable" woman has more information than I have. "The area in which the canopy was found was further searched for other traces of wreckage."

KATE: But that has to be good. I mean, they were out searching again.

MOIRA: They're not searching now, and the point is that I still don't know where the canopy frame was found. I don't know under what circumstances it was found. I don't know anything about any search that was conducted for "other traces of wreckage." And the fact remains, those National Defence bastards made me a solemn promise /when they turfed us out of Married Quarters.

KATE: I know I know I know — You'd be the first to hear any juicy tidbit and promises do not fucking expire with the passage of time!

MOIRA: I beg /your pardon?!

KATE: I've heard it all a billion times. Mum, I can't take this shit anymore.

KATE exits, WIND swirls and screams outside the window and—

Scene Eighteen

KATE circles back. It's 2017. She's still piecing memories together.

KATE: Another five years fly by.

MOIRA, with pen and paper, paces. Window is open. Sound of restless WIND outside.

KATE: *(Enters.)* Any luck?

MOIRA: It's in *(Gestures to her head.)* here, but I can't seem to get it down on paper.

KATE: That's not like my mum. She writes killer letters.

MOIRA: I'm frightened, Kate. I think I'm losing my mind.

KATE: No. Hey, I've got an idea. What if you dictate and I record?

MOIRA: That could take the rest of my life. You ain't no stenographer, kid, and my voice sure ain't what it used to be.

KATE offers up the tiny recorder.

KATE: Voila.

MOIRA: Dinky little thing. Looks like a toy.

KATE: I carry it with me in case I have a brilliant idea when I'm out walking or when I can't face the blank page or because I'm afraid I'll forget something. What do you say? Just let 'er rip and then you can revise, if needed… Mum?

MOIRA: Turn it on.

KATE does. MOIRA refers to a document as she dictates. She has some hesitation in finding names, words, the correct amount of money billed, etc. as she reads, but her ideas flow remarkably well.

Colonel M. Legrand
April 23, 1997
Director of Flight Safety
ETC.

Dear Sir:

I received a bill from Purolator Courier Ltd. in the amount of $18.56. Initially, I was puzzled. When I realized that I was being billed for the Flight Safety Report of an accident which… which deprived me of my husband and our two children of their father and a secure family life over 41 years ago … well…

I am sending this bill to you to do with as you wish. Billing me for a copy of a report of the accident which, which… so diminished our lives is insensitive and hurtful. My daughter is hurt. I am hurt. Nobody can hurt my son — he is dead.

I am enclosing a self-addressed stamped envelope in case you wish to contact me. Please DO NOT telephone. Stress has left me with vocal problems. When I am anxious I lose my voice — nothing physical, I'm told — just the holding in of too much grief.

Yours truly, etc.

KATE: Oh Mum…

MOIRA: Too much?

KATE: Up yours, Mr. Flight Safety.

Scene Nineteen

It's October 23, 2017. Again, KATE is alone in the house with files, etc.

YOUNG MARY'S VOICE: Air Craft Flash!

OLD MARY'S VOICE: It's years before I learn that a jet out of Comox went missing that day, the 22nd of March, 1956. Just disappeared from the sky. Kate, it was your father's jet I saw fly over. I made the call.

KATE: But no one was listening.

October 8, 2017. Round two in the Callaghan Valley.

CHRIS appears, bringing Callaghan Valley Base Camp with him. KATE is with him.

KATE: I remember hiding behind a book or fleeing the house whenever "The Vic Stories" started up. I don't remember initiating a single conversation about my father's disappearance.

I don't remember reading any of the documents that Mum fought so hard to get her hands on. God, I just didn't get it. The RCAF volunteered nothing. Ever. Mum finally had to go through Freedom of Information to get those reports.

I do remember thinking Dad, or maybe Darryl James, screwed up, or that the weather took them down.

CHRIS: Don't buy it. The weather sucked that day, but not bad enough to bring down a fighter jet piloted by two experienced RCAF officers, and especially not the T33. Those planes were tough, maneuverable. They flew them in the big air shows.

KATE: I know that now. Finally doing my homework. I got my hands on a copy of the Department of National Defence Investigative Report on the crash site discovered up here last August.

CHRIS: Yes! Spill.

KATE: The plane glided in like a big, winged sled on deep snow. Minimal impact, minimal damage. There was no evidence — zero — to suggest mechanical failure or pilot error. And wait for it… the Feds' analysis proves the plane's engine died due to fuel starvation.

CHRIS: The tank was empty?

KATE: Yeah.

CHRIS: Holy shit.

KATE: Yeah. And based on what the experts in Ottawa have to say to explain the mystery of the empty tank, it looks like it wasn't fuelled sufficiently — or at all — before our pilots left the Comox Base. I think that means someone else screwed up. And got away with it.

Scene Twenty

And it's October 2016. WIND blows up and waves slap against rocks. We're back at the ocean in Victoria. MOIRA and KATE drink cocoa right where we left them.

MOIRA: If there's a god he must be some joker. Your father left his face behind... After Stevie's birth I, oh lord, for weeks, maybe months I could barely look at him. And he knew. Oh yes /he did.

KATE: No, he didn't.

MOIRA: My baby boy could see right through his mad bitch of a mummy.

KATE: Get over yourself.

MOIRA: Sometimes I think I never really saw him. That I never really forgave my sweet boy for not being his father.

KATE: And there it is. After all these years. What do you want me to say?

MOIRA: /Nothing.

KATE: "It's all right, Mum"?

MOIRA: Do you think I don't know it's not all right? My god, I was actually afraid to say those words to you. Always watching me, judging me.

KATE: No!

MOIRA: Even as a child.

KATE: Well, somebody had to look after you.

MOIRA: So serious. Always trying to keep the lid on.

KATE: Okay, so what do you want from me now?

MOIRA: What I've always wanted. I want you to spend some time with your father.

Beat.

MOIRA: I want you to get to know him.

KATE: And how exactly would you recommend I do that?

MOIRA: Talk to him. It will do you the world of good.

KATE: You mean talk like praying?

MOIRA: I talk to him every day.

KATE: Yup. And he's dead.

MOIRA: Vic will never be dead to me.

KATE: So you're saying he's here with us now.

MOIRA: Yes.

KATE: Like a ghost?

MOIRA: I prefer spirit.

KATE: Stop this.

MOIRA: There's nothing to be afraid of.

KATE: I'm worried about you.

MOIRA: You should be worrying about those blinders you welded on after Stevie's death.

KATE: That's enough. I mean it.

MOIRA: Vic's visitation to/night was

KATE: His what?!

MOIRA: This is not the first time he's appeared /in your presence.

KATE: Holy shit. Are we talking Jesus Christ here?

MOIRA: Don't be an ass.

KATE: So just your garden variety apparition or miracle then.

MOIRA: What would you call it?

KATE: Hallucinations? Wishful thinking? Dementia. Time to take you in for another check-up, old lady.

MOIRA: Oh Katie, you need to take a good, hard look in the mirror. Cruelty is making you ugly.

KATE: All right, so I'm ugly. But what's this "get to know your father" stuff all about? Really? What do you deep down in your guts want from me, Mum? Forgiveness?

MOIRA: You bet, but I'm not expecting that'll be coming around the mountain anytime soon.

KATE: Oh my god, this is about going up that mountain /again.

MOIRA: What I want is for you to stop treating me like a child, like someone who's lost her mind and her right to freedom of thought and loving and living as her will and heart dictate.

KATE: I won't be responsible for taking you up / that mountain.

MOIRA: Just talk to your father. Please.

KATE: I'm not playing this game.

MOIRA: Why not? You talk to Stevie.

KATE: I do not.

MOIRA: All the time. And he talks to you.

KATE: He's not talking to me. He's camping in my head. Memories, Mum. No ghost.

MOIRA: Do you have the guts to admit that your brother and your father are here with us now?

KATE: Stevie's been residing in *(Gestures to her head.)* here all my life. But that's all it is, because in this moment, there is you and there is me and we have the night sky and the Pacific Ocean and our precious memories and our love and our stupid Irish guilt and that's all there is.

MOIRA: Will you just for once try a leap of faith? For yourself. For Stevie and your father.

KATE: They're dead.

MOIRA: We're family. That's a fact of life that death can never change. Please.

Beat.

KATE: Stevie? Come out… come out wherever—

STEVIE is suddenly very present.

KATE: I don't know how to do this.

MOIRA: Just talk.

KATE: Maybe I need to get down on my knees and beg his forgiveness.

MOIRA: For what?

KATE: For winning the lottery. For surviving long enough to become Good Old Reliable But Oh So Disappointing Kate.

MOIRA: You're not disappointing, but you had a hard time of it, both of you. I will always feel responsible for that.

KATE: Because everything that happened was your fault?

MOIRA: Because I'm your mother.

KATE: I'll give this leap-of-faith-thing a shot if you'll drop that big bag of martyr shit you've been dragging around since Dad plummeted out of our lives.

MOIRA: You're terrified.

KATE: No, yes, no goddammit. I'm sick to death of this. All these years, the same thing over and over and over and over and over and over. You are not responsible for everything that happened. Get it? We made choices. Stevie and me. There are days I wonder… Did you know I was at a party when I was fifteen where someone was shot? Some deranged biker dude's in the house chewing pieces of glass and waving a gun around his head and I just keep on dancing and drinking and toking my way through the night.

MOIRA: None of this / matters now.

KATE: But Stevie, man, he was the master of bad choices. Crank yourself up with non-stop booze and pills and needles, and life looks a whole lot sweeter, baby. Until the needles are dirty and your body craps out… Are you listening to this, Stevie?

MOIRA: When did you become so angry and… rigid?

KATE: Years ago. Where were you? Shacked up with your ghost, that's where. I should have left you there, but I couldn't stand it anymore. I couldn't stand Stevie's lies, his stealing, his overdoses, his car crashes, his throwing himself off a third-storey balcony not once, but twice, his trying to hang himself in /the garage.

MOIRA: No! He didn't. You're lying. No no /no!

KATE: Yes, yes yes. I come up the driveway after a party and have this, I don't know, premonition? Or maybe it's a miracle. I go into the garage and pretty much smack right into his legs, swinging back and forth. I don't even know how I get him down or what happens afterwards. Sometimes I think I must be inventing this shit because it's all too vague and shadowy and awful. How do you forget, how do I forget the details of something, someone so important?

MOIRA: Shhh shhhh.

KATE: I couldn't stand what he was doing to you. But most of all I couldn't stand watching my brother disappear. I didn't know where he was, who he was anymore. So I let him go. What kind of stupid bitch ditches her little brother, her oldest best friend, the one she played horsies and forts with and the Flintstones and rebelled against you with and smoked weed with in the Ross Bay Cemetery /when we snuck out at night?

MOIRA: Katie, stop this now.

KATE: I should never have talked you into that holiday, but I was afraid you were going to break. I knew I was breaking. And I hoped if we got away we'd both be able to breathe a little easier and that maybe we'd laugh together again.

MOIRA: We did laugh.

KATE: I… God, I didn't know he was so far along.

MOIRA: He didn't want us to know.

KATE: I should have made it my business to find out. I should have made sure you were there with him in that hospital when he died. I should have been there with him.

STEVIE is close by. He holds and strokes a small tabby cat.

MOIRA: Stevie's free. Has been for … thirty years. And he made damn good and sure we knew.

A grey and cloudy afternoon thirty years earlier sails in on the WIND, transporting KATE and MOIRA to a beach farther north on Vancouver Island, near Campbell River. They take stock of their surroundings.

MOIRA: So this is Stevie's Beach.

KATE: He made himself a nest here, with an ocean view.

MOIRA: And an island across the way. Beautiful.

KATE: Lonely.

MOIRA: What will happen to his lovely kitties? Kate, I can't remember their names.

Beat.

KATE: Are you ready?

MOIRA: No.

KATE: Take my hand.

They walk into the frigid, grey water up to their calves. KATE opens a bag and, in silence, they sprinkle STEVIE's ashes into the Pacific Ocean. Immediately, clouds part like curtains over the water. Sun streaks through, for just a moment, and—

KATE: Mum… look up.

The sound of a great blue heron.

MOIRA: Oh, oh…

They watch as clouds close back up and sun and heron disappear. And it's 2016 again. KATE and MOIRA are right where we left them that night on the Victoria beach. STEVIE and his tabby cat are nearby.

MOIRA: Look at me.

KATE: Yes, I talk to Stevie. But I can't reach him. I can't touch him.

MOIRA: Give me your hand, sweetheart.

KATE does and MOIRA places it over KATE's heart.

MOIRA: Our sweet boy is right here. And *(MOIRA's heart.)* here.

And STEVIE disappears. Then MOIRA places KATE's hand on different parts of MOIRA's body: perhaps her thinning hair or a breast, her face, her own shaking, ravaged hands.

MOIRA: This and—

KATE: What are you / doing?

MOIRA: Shhh. And this and these, this is what the end of life feels like. My life.

KATE: Mum, no.

MOIRA: It may not be pretty, and it sure as hell ain't for sissies, but it's a fact, and I'm here now, and there's only one way out.

KATE: Mum, no—

MOIRA: Kid, what you need to understand is that I'm finally where I want to be.

KATE: Oh god.

MOIRA: Of course you're frightened. But this is happening to me. And you can't change it. But you can help me.

KATE: Mum, please—

MOIRA: Take me up that mountain.

WIND blows up bringing—

Scene Twenty-One

The Callaghan Valley with it. CHRIS SEERS appears leading MOIRA and KATE.

WIND builds throughout the scene.

MOIRA: Stop here.

CHRIS: Everything okay?

MOIRA: Yes.

KATE: What's going on?

MOIRA: We need to stop here.

KATE: Mum?

CHRIS: It's gonna get dark soon.

MOIRA: For a moment or two. Please.

CHRIS: Water?

MOIRA: No.

KATE: Okay, let's say Dad and Darryl James really were somewhere nearby... They eat their sardines and biscuits. And then what? They just walk away and leave behind a mini Last Supper tableau?

MOIRA: Here comes the wind. I knew it, I knew it.

WIND begins to gust up.

KATE: *(To CHRIS.)* Doesn't that seem strange to you? I mean, wouldn't they have packed their cups and spoons and knives out?

CHRIS: Maybe something happened, and they had to move fast... Snow must have been piled up to their chests in places. And they weren't dressed for that kind of weather.

KATE: Knives would have been useful.

CHRIS: They were trained to look for a creek, any water source, and follow it down.

KATE: Parachute cord would have been useful.

CHRIS: Look, ladies, we gotta motor. Let's focus on getting back. We can speculate all you like at the Lodge.

Sounds of building WIND and creaking trees.

WIND: Heeeeere… heeeeeeere… heeeeeeere…

MOIRA: Listen.

CHRIS: The wind in these mountains can be a bitch. Hell, I've seen her gust up out of nowhere, lift a man right off his feet and toss him like a twig.

WIND: Heeeeeere…

MOIRA: I knew it I knew it I knew it.

WIND: Heeeeeeeere… Heeeeeeere…./Heeeeeere…

MOIRA: He's here. Here!

MOIRA stands to search.

KATE: Mum?! Stay where you are.

The sound of movement, cracking branches, gunshot loud, breaks through the sound of the WIND.

KATE: What was that?!

CHRIS: Quiet. And stand still.

A GRIZZLY BEAR has moved into the area. Growly-snuffling can be heard.

KATE: *(Whispers.)* Grizzly?

CHRIS: Shhh.

They look at GRIZZLY BEAR for what feels like forever. Then—

MOIRA: Look up.

KATE: *(Whispering, holding onto MOIRA.)* Mum!

CHRIS: Shhh! Nobody moves or talks.

GRIZZLY BEAR steps closer, rises on hind legs. KATE and CHRIS are rigid, like stone, but MOIRA is strangely peaceful. Finally, GRIZZLY turns and leaves.

CHRIS: Fuck.

KATE: Uh huh…

CHRIS: That was one fucked-up close encounter. What the fuck, Moira? You could have got us fucking killed… I've had a few run-ins with grizzlies in my time, hard to avoid, them being top of the food chain and pretty much everywhere up here, but I have never, never experienced anything like that. Did you look into her eyes? I swear, that old sow was trying to tell us something.

Snap out of it, ladies.

KATE is still, silent. MOIRA is moving now, scanning the trees around them.

We're running out of light.

MOIRA: Look up. Up.

The tattered remains of a leather parachute harness and parachute cord swing from a tree branch. WIND gusts, and a battered, old flight helmet is dislodged from its perch. It tumbles to the ground, some of it breaks apart. CHRIS reaches for it.

MOIRA: No!

She examines it. CHRIS notes location coordinates and prepares to bag up the helmet.

KATE: Careful.

CHRIS: It's falling apart, Moira, real fragile, maybe I should—

MOIRA: Vic.

KATE: We don't know that yet.

CHRIS: Let me take this now.

KATE: Give it to Chris, Mum.

CHRIS: I'll bag it up and treat it like the Holy Grail.

MOIRA: I've found you.

CHRIS packs up helmet and manages to bring the harness and cord down and pack them away. WIND escorts them out of the area.

Scene Twenty-Two

It is night in a room in the lodge where the helmet has been placed. MOIRA is alone. She reaches out and gently touches the helmet. To her, the crushed and shattered object truly does have the significance of the Holy Grail.

As MOIRA talks and embraces the helmet, VIC materializes in his flying uniform and wearing the helmet as it once was, the way he looked before he climbed into that plane on March 22, 1956. For the first time, they can make physical contact.

MOIRA: This helmet is whole again. I'm unbuckling the chin-strap and lifting it from your head. I can't help myself; I bury my nose in your hair and … *(She inhales.)* Home, sweet home. And now I'm stroking your hair. I am. My fingers are straight and strong and nimble. I run them over the ridge of your cheekbone to the stubble on your jaw, but these fingers have minds of their own. They make a beeline for your lips… oh. You see what you're doing to me? One night with you and I'm ready to slip out of this wreck of a body. You and me lying together up here with the grizzly bears. And why the hell not? At least one of them is on our side.

A haunting version of 'It's Not for Me to Say' plays. MOIRA and VIC dance to their song.

MOIRA: I have missed dancing with you, husband. I figured we'd have to learn all over again. Was I wrong or was I wrong, baby? Just like riding a bicycle. Our bodies fitting together just so and then moving together just so. Lock step, lock hips, lock lips. /Just so.

And they're gone.

Moira (Clarice McCord) and ghost of Vic (Darrian Gaetz) dance to their song.

Scene Twenty-Three

KATE lights a candle. She is as she was at the top of the play, but the files and papers and photographs are mainly packed away. There are two attractive boxes with her: a jewellery box and a container for ashes.

KATE: I found you before anyone else was up the next morning. One year ago today. You were lying on the floor, curled around the helmet. A dead woman spooning her lover. I like to think he'd taken you in the night. You looked ridiculously beautiful. Hello, Victor. Goodbye, grief. Goodbye, rage. Goodbye, Mum #3.

Kate opens the small box to reveal a tiny fragment of helmet.

KATE: Shh. I'm a thief. Just this one tiny piece.

The rest of the helmet and the harness and parachute cord will end up in some air force museum. Maybe on the Comox Base. Maybe there'll be an exhibit. Maybe it will make headlines and people will come in droves and marvel at the unresolved mystery of the two lost pilots. Or maybe in a few months the exhibit will grow stale, the museum staff will take it down and pack up what's left of them and file it away on some dusty storeroom shelf.

But not if I can help it.

KATE scoops a small portion of MOIRA's ashes from the wooden box and sprinkles them over the piece of helmet in the other box. She shuts the box, cradles it, then closes her eyes. A moment of stillness and silence.

KATE: You were right, Mum. Dad survived that crash. He was on that mountain. Alive and fighting to get back home… To his family.

A sound like WIND exhaling. The house is silent and still. KATE watches through the window as WIND puffs up and playfully buffets the tree in the fading afternoon light.

End of Play

Gerald Stubbs
1924 – 1956

Glossary

"Aircraft Flash" — during the Cold War, this expression was used to indicate that the person calling needed to report the sighting of an aircraft flying overhead immediately. Individuals living in some areas of Canada's Pacific Coast were designated as responders, e.g., in Pemberton.

Aircraft Canopy — transparent enclosure over cockpits of some types of aircraft provides a controlled environment for aircraft occupants and allows for a greater field of view. In an emergency the canopy is ejected before pilots / crew are able to eject.

Cold War — The Cold War began 1947 and ended 1991. A period of geopolitical tension between the Soviet Union and the United States, and their respective allies, the Eastern Bloc and the Western Bloc.

Ejection Seats — designed to rescue pilot or other crew (primarily military) during flight emergencies, seats are often propelled by an explosive charge, taking pilots with them.

Fuselage — main body section of an aircraft.

Gimli — a community in Manitoba's Interlake region north of Winnipeg. The first European settlers were Icelandic. Gimli maintains strong ties with Iceland.

Jitterbug — athletic dance for couples popularized by African Americans in the USA early in the 20th century. Associated with swing dance, e.g., Lindy Hop and jive.

RCAF — Royal Canadian Air Force, part of National Defence and Canadian Armed Forces.

Tasmanian Devil — in *Our Ghosts,* an animated character in Warner Bros' *Looney Tunes* and *Merrie Melodies* cartoons. Irrational and moves like a tornado: fast and in circles.

T-33 Silver Star (also known as T-Bird) — was one of the most maneuverable and fast fighter jets in the air force at the time. It travelled at just under the speed of sound — 760 miles per hour.

Whistler SAR — Whistler Search and Rescue Society is a non-profit organization based in Whistler, BC. Its primary function is as a community resource to assist the RCMP in a variety of search and rescue functions.

Afterword

Our Ghosts, Our Stories

As Sally's friend and colleague, I've been blessed to have witnessed the growth of the script for *Our Ghosts* from initial seedling to its current fully realized bountiful, blooming form.

When Sally first told me the incredible story of how her father, Flying Officer Gerald Stubbs, and his coworker went missing and the resultant decades of anguish the family suffered, my playwright's antennae went up. A father whose plane goes down but whose body is never recovered, a mother who refuses to relinquish the search for his remains at the cost of her emotional well-being, and two children who are robbed not only of a father they never knew, but also in many ways a mother too. Clearly this story has the makings of a drama of epic Shakespearean proportions.

All Sally had to do was write it.

It's not enough for a playwright to have a good story in her back pocket; she has to make it "play." This is, after all, the job of the dramatist. The writer is faced with a particularly steep mountain to climb when writing a story from her own life. This is especially true with stories about family.

One of the biggest challenges in writing our own stories is dealing with that age-old question, "What will so-and-so think about what I have to say?" Even when we decide to forge ahead regardless, we're still going to hear their voices in our heads, even—and perhaps especially—the voices of those who have passed on. This concern is not a light one. Just as Moira says about Vic, so too we might say of these voices that they "will never be dead to me." To quote Faulkner, "The past is never dead. It's not even past." And writing a play about your mother? Come on. Forget climbing a mountain. Point me to the summit and I'll jump!

But Sally manages to pull off this tremendous feat with aplomb. She pays beautiful tribute to her mother, Claire Stubbs, not by creating the character of Moira as saintly, in fact far from it. Both Moira and Sally's stand-in, Kate, are fully fleshed, living, breathing characters with flaws and foibles who not only struggle with the forces impinging on them, but with each other as well. Moira asks, "Is this never going to end?" and Kate replies, "Oh, it's going to end. You have my word on it." But to what precisely does "this" refer? Of course, the characters are talking about the never-ending lack of answers with regard to the disappearance, but there is much more going on here. The struggle that exists between mother and daughter is every bit as dynamic as their struggle with bureaucracy. In fact, it is more potent because their bond is cemented in love. Good drama thrives on conflict that is immediate and with high stakes. *Our Ghosts* delivers in spades.

At one point, Kate says, "I feel like if I turn around quickly, I'll find Stevie, but always just slightly out of reach . . .," a sentiment that could just as easily describe the act of writing. Sometimes as writers we think we have something pinned down only to have it slip from our grasp. The act of writing is a journey of discovery, often one that yields more questions than answers. But this is a good thing. After all, it is the job of the playwright to ask questions.

Sally's writing for discovery mirrors Kate's and Moira's quest for the truth. But facts alone do not truth make, and if not handled well, will impede the narrative's forward motion—a death knell to a play. Not that one seeks to eliminate facts from the story—God is in the details, after all. But in structuring a play it arguably always will be the case that facts will have to be altered in *some* way. The biggest challenge lies in deciding which facts are necessary and which are not. *Our Ghosts* contains just enough information to properly pay homage to the real-life story that so defined Sally's family without interfering with the crafting of compelling drama.

Oftentimes we write our stories as a way to discover possibility. Claire passed away not knowing how her husband met his death. While Sally was unable to deliver on a two-fold promise of providing answers in her mother's lifetime and taking Claire's ashes to the site where Gerald perished, she is able to do so through the character of Kate and in writing this play. As Moira says, "Promises do not expire with the passage of time." *Our Ghosts* is a promise delivered by a daughter to a mother, albeit in a different form.

To borrow and alter Carrie Fisher's words on writing our stories, Sally has taken her mother's broken heart and turned it into art.

— *Sherry MacDonald*

The Mystery of Flight 21454
By Steve LeClair

On March 22, 1956, Royal Canadian Air Force Flight 21454 left its base in Comox, BC at approximately 9:40 am to conduct a routine instrument practice flight. This was more than a decade after World War II, in which the West Coast played a vital role in the Pacific theatre of war. The aircraft was piloted by Flight Officers Gerald S. Stubbs and James E. Miller of the 409 Tactical Fighter Squadron. This training flight was supposed to last approximately one hour. The T-33 Silver Star, or "T-Bird," one of the fastest jets in the air force at the time, cruised at just under the speed of sound — 760 miles an hour. That day the pilots were to fly a box pattern heading east, then south, before turning back toward Comox.

At 10:17 am, the plane was last sighted on radar entering bad weather. At this time, the plane was approximately 15 miles east of Comox heading toward base. The plane disappeared from radar and all attempts to contact the aircraft by radio were negative.

An extensive search was conducted at the time to locate James Miller and Gerald Stubbs over an area of 4,500 square miles. No evidence of the aircraft or crew was found.

Both pilots were married with young families. It would take eighteen years before any evidence of the aircraft was located.

In November 1974, hikers found the canopy of the aircraft in the Callaghan Valley on a ridge. The Royal Canadian Air Force conducted a search of the area. Details of this search were vague other than the fact that no further evidence was found.

In August of 1997, the wreckage (the right wing and the fuselage) of the aircraft was located and reported by a firefighting crew flying over the area. RCAF attended the scene and after an examination, it was determined that the aircraft engine failed in flight due to fuel starvation. A third search was conducted;

however, this search did not reveal the presence of ejection seats, any human remains or additional evidence.

In October of 2010, two employees of a backcountry ski lodge were out for a hike and located an old flight helmet covered in moss. There were markings on the helmet that matched what was used by pilots of the 409 Squadron from the time that Miller and Stubbs went missing. The helmet was turned over to the RCMP, who opened a missing persons case.

Police located daughters of both missing pilots and obtained DNA samples from them should any human remains ever be found.

In October 2011 a ground search was conducted in the area that the helmet was found. The search was conducted by numerous Search and Rescue teams from Whistler and the surrounding area; however, no evidence was found. Additional searches were conducted by Whistler SAR every year except for 2013 when an early snowfall blanketed the search area.

In 2019, WSAR made a significant discovery, finding a major portion of the wreckage, the left wing of the aircraft, which was dramatically off course from the original site where the fuselage was located earlier.

The RCMP file into the case remains open. Police remain in contact with the daughters of both pilots, keeping them updated on search efforts. Whistler Search and Rescue continues to search the area to locate any further evidence, specifically, any human remains and the ejection seats. Whistler Search and Rescue incorporates the search into their regular training schedule. WSAR continued search and training efforts are now focused in the area of Callaghan FSR and the creek, south of the lake.

The search continues to this day, carried out by local search and rescue volunteers, Whistler Search & Rescue, and the RCMP — all determined to bring closure to this case, and peace to the families.

The Facts

- On **March 22, 1956**, RCAF Comox Flyer Officers James Miller and Gerald Stubbs set flight from Comox at 9:48 AM in a Silver Star (T-33), a military training jet. The officers were briefed to carry out an instrument flying practice that was to last 1.5 hours.
- **9:57 AM**: The pilot communicated that they were at an altitude of 25,000 ft. This was the last transmission received.
- **10:15 AM**: The aircraft was tracked by radar within 15 miles of Comox.
- **10:17 AM:** The aircraft disappeared from the radar due to weather interference. All attempts to further radio contact the plane were negative.
- **March 22 – April 6, 1956:** An extensive search was conducted to locate James Miller and Gerald Stubbs over an area of 4,500 square miles. No evidence of the aircraft or crew was found.
- **November, 1974:** Hikers located the canopy of the aircraft in the Callaghan Valley. A search of the area was conducted; however, details of this search were vague other than the fact that no further evidence was found.
- **Late 1980s:** An abandoned rustic campsite was located in the Callaghan Valley near a stream. The campsite included a bench, sardine cans, and a parachute cord. However, the individual who found the campsite was unaware of the previous discovery of the T-33 canopy and assumed that the camp had been occupied by prospectors many years before. Could the campsite have been occupied by one or both of the missing pilots? Unfortunately, searchers have been unable to locate this camp again.
- **August, 1997:** The wreckage (the right wing and the fuselage) of the aircraft was located. After an examination, it was determined that the aircraft engine failed in flight due to fuel starvation. A third search was conducted. The search was unsuccessful.
- **October, 2010:** A flight helmet was found in the Callaghan Valley.

- **October 2011:** A ground search was conducted in the area where the helmet was found. The search was conducted by numerous Search and Rescue teams from the area and the RCMP. No evidence was found.

- Additional searches were conducted by Whistler Search and Rescue in 2014 and every year thereafter.

- **In 2019**, WSAR made a significant discovery, finding a major portion of the wreckage, that being the left wing of the aircraft, which was dramatically off course from the original site where the fuselage was located earlier.

- **Today**: The RCMP file into the case remains open. Whistler Search and Rescue will continue to search the area to locate any further evidence; specifically, any human remains and the ejection seats. Whistler Search and Rescue incorporates the search into their regular trainings. WSAR continued search and training efforts are now focused in the area of Callaghan FSR and the creek, south of the lake.

Comox RCAF Base entrance, Comox, BC. (archival photo)

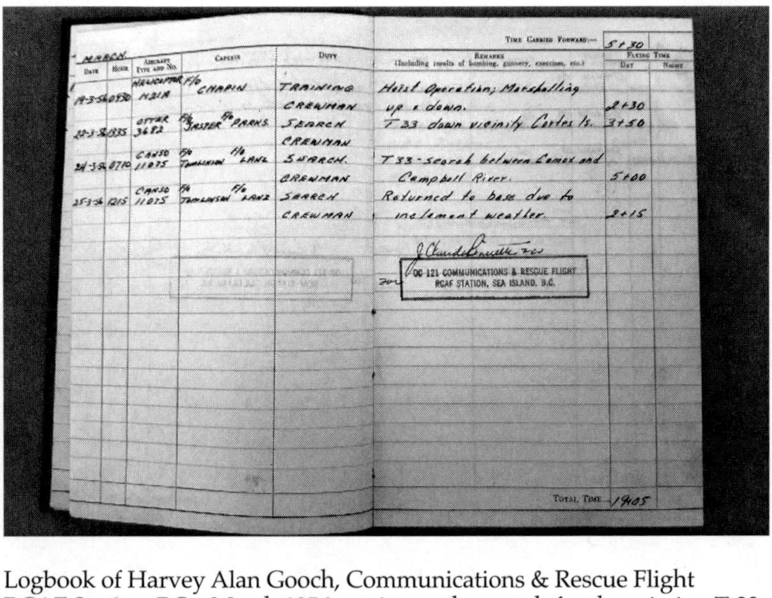

Time Carried Forward:— 5+30

MARCH

Date	Hour	Aircraft Type and No.	Captain	Duty	Remarks (Including results of bombing, gunnery, exercises, etc.)	Flying Time Day	Flying Time Night
19-3-56	0930	HELICOPTER H21A	F/O CHAPIN	TRAINING CREWMAN	Hoist Operation; Marshalling up & down.	2+30	
22-3-56	1335	OTTER 3682	F/O JASPER F/O PARKS	SEARCH CREWMAN	T33 down vicinity Cortes Is.	3+50	
24-3-56	0710	CANSO 11075	F/O TOMLINSON F/O LANE	SEARCH CREWMAN	T33 - search between Comox and Campbell River.	5+00	
25-3-56	1215	CANSO 11075	F/O TOMLINSON F/O LANE	SEARCH CREWMAN	Returned to base due to inclement weather.	2+15	

OC 121 COMMUNICATIONS & RESCUE FLIGHT
RCAF STATION, SEA ISLAND, B.C.

Total Time 19+05

Logbook of Harvey Alan Gooch, Communications & Rescue Flight RCAF Station, BC – March 1956 entries on the search for the missing T-33 thought then to have gone down near Cortes Island. (photo by Jay Gooch)

Search area overview of Callaghan Valley. In1974, hikers discovered the T-33 454 aircraft canopy in the area. (WSAR photo)

Remains of a 409 Squadron flight helmet were found in 2010 by two staff members of a backcountry ski lodge in the Callaghan Valley. They turned it over to Whistler RCMP, who then opened a missing persons file. (Whistler RCMP photo)

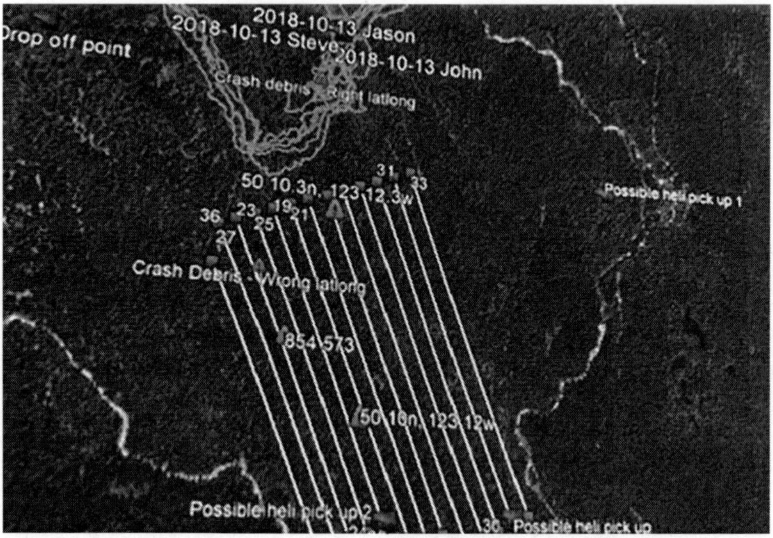

2018 T-33 Search Tracking Map. Callaghan Valley. (WSAR photo)

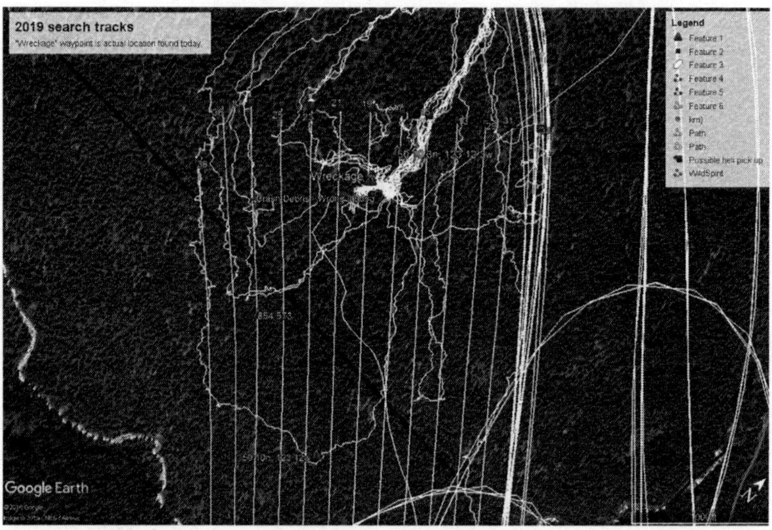

2019 T-33 Search Tracks – tracking map that WSAR team plots and uses as a reference, shows actual site of wreckage found 2019, Callaghan Valley. (WSAR photo)

2019 find. Whistler SAR Society volunteer seen with remains of left wing of T-33. (WSAR photo)

2019 find. Brad Sills, President, Whistler SAR Society, and all WSAR members involved in search seen with left wing of T-33. Find was far off-course from site where right wing and fuselage was located by firefighting crew flying over the area in 1997. (WSAR photo)

Claire Stubbs
September 9, 1926 to December 23, 2017

In 1958, Claire packed her two-year-old son Jerry and his four-year-old sister Sally into an old Pontiac and drove away from Winnipeg and her family and friends. They were heading back to Comox, BC, where Flying Officer Gerald Stephen Stubbs, Claire's husband and Sally and Jerry's dad, was last seen just over two years earlier. On March 22nd, 1956 he and his co-pilot took off from the Comox Air Base on a routine training flight which mysteriously disappeared. At the time, she was carrying Jerry. Sally was a toddler. Shortly after Jerry was born they were ordered out of Married Quarters and moved off the Base.

Driving off the ferry, Claire realized that living in the Comox area would be too painful and made the decision to head to Victoria. It was close enough that she would hear about and be able to respond quickly to any developments relating to the missing plane and pilots. For months, even years, she refused to admit that her beloved was dead. And she never stopped searching for the answers to her questions about his disappearance. How? What? Where? Why? She never remarried. She never wanted to remarry.

Claire began a relentless process of research, including letter writing, phone calls and meetings with bureaucrats and politicians, and requisitioning official files under the Freedom of Information Act. The plane's canopy was finally discovered decades later in the wild Callaghan Valley, hundreds of miles away from where the official search had taken place. Several years after that, the wreckage of the body of the plane was found in the same general area. There was no evidence discovered to reveal the whereabouts of the missing pilots. Still Claire held onto the belief that her love's resting place would be found.

Claire struggled to raise and care for her children on a stenographer's salary. In an era where there was no such thing as daycare and a woman was unable even to take out a mortgage without having a man co-sign for her, she worked like a fiend and cherished the support of her mom and dad, who moved from Winnipeg to be near and help. She even managed to purchase her own home. Along the way she won the respect of her colleagues and employers and made some great friends. She also suffered losses including, in one tough year, the early deaths of her "soul-sister," Elaine, and her beautiful and loving son, Jerry.

Claire was as feisty and independent as they come. Despite her failing health in the last decade of her life, she was victorious in her final battle. Adamant that she would remain in her home, she did just that until the day before the end of her life.

Claire was loving and empathetic. Her smile was electric. She loved to crank up her tunes and drive up the Island or dance alone in her living room, which she did well into her 80s. She had a quiet and wicked sense of humour, a soft heart, and unwavering faith in those she loved. And if — when — the mystery of Claire's beloved's disappearance is solved, her daughter, Sally, will keep the promise she made to her mom and lay her ashes at her dad's final resting place.